CLASSIC GARDEN STRUCTURES

CLASSIC GARDEN STRUCTURES

18 ELEGANT PROJECTS

to

ENHANCE YOUR GARDEN

Jan *&* Michael Gertley

The Taunton Press

Taunton
BOOKS & VIDEOS
for fellow enthusiasts

Printed in the United States of America
10 9 8 7 6 5 4 3 2 1

The Taunton Press, Inc., 63 South Main Street,
PO Box 5506, Newtown, CT 06470-5506
e-mail: tp@taunton.com

Distributed by Publishers Group West

Library of Congress Cataloging-in-Publication Data

Gertley, Jan.
    Classic garden structures : 18 elegant projects to
enhance your garden / Jan and Michael Gertley.
        p.   cm.
    Includes bibliographical references.
    ISBN 1-56158-241-7
    1. Woodwork–Amateurs' manuals. 2. Garden ornaments
and furniture–Design and construction–Amateurs' manuals.
3. Garden structures–Design and construction–Amateurs'
manuals. 4. Gardening–Equipment and supplies–Design and
construction–Amateurs' manuals. I. Gertley, Michael.
II. Title.
TT185.G46   1998
684.1'8–dc21   98-12028
                                                   CIP

About Your Safety

Working with wood is inherently dangerous. Using hand or power tools improperly or ignoring standard safety practices can lead to permanent injury or even death. Don't try to perform operations you learn about here (or elsewhere) unless you're certain they are safe for you. If something about an operation doesn't feel right, don't do it. Look for another way. We want you to enjoy the craft, so please keep safety foremost in your mind whenever you're in the shop.

To our fathers and grandfathers,

whose tutelage and genes gave us

our love of working with wood

ACKNOWLEDGMENTS

We are grateful to the terrific staff at The Taunton Press
for their participation in this project.
The entire staff, including Helen Albert, Cherilyn DeVries,
Diane Sinitsky, Lynne Phillips, and many others,
gave their support, creative talents, and hours of work
to make this book a reality. We thank you all!

CONTENTS

INTRODUCTION   2

1   Tools and Materials   4
TOOLS   7
WOODS   16
FASTENERS   18
FINISHES   20

2   Trellises and Plant Supports   22
TOMATO TRELLIS   24
BERRY TRELLIS   32
POLE BEAN TRELLIS   38
PLANTER BOX AND OBELISK   44

3   Tables, Benches, and Plant Stands   54
GREENHOUSE TABLE   56
POTTING BENCH   64
ROLLING BENCH   70
POTTED PLANT STAND   78
VEGETABLE WASHSTAND   84

4 Structures for Growing Plants   94

RAISED BED   96

COLD FRAME   102

STRAWBERRY TOWER   112

GREENHOUSE   118

5 Garden Tools and Accessories   142

GARDEN SIEVE   144

LINE AND REEL ROW MARKER   148

PLANT CADDY   154

FLAT AND FLAT DIBBLE   160

SEED SAVER'S BOX   166

GLOSSARY   176

RESOURCES   178

PROJECT RESOURCES   179

BIBLIOGRAPHY   181

METRIC EQUIVALENCE CHART   183

INTRODUCTION

For weekend gardeners, as well as for avid horticulturists, gardens provide an unlimited source of beauty and inspiration. We expend a great deal of time and energy coaxing nature into the various landscapes we have pictured in our minds. But nature is not the only skilled craftsman at work; it is often man-made structures that help define a particular garden style.

Decorative architectural details that were once common around the turn of the century have all but disappeared from today's construction. It's hard for most home builders to justify the added expense of decorative trim moldings or shuttered windows. The designs of garden structures and accessories have also suffered from the modern trend of basic designs distributed *en masse*. Today, more often than not, we see form running a distant second to function. Sometimes, the only way to reclaim some of that lost potential is by picking up a hammer and saw.

There are many rewards to building projects yourself. Variety, for example, is a strong benefit. A large selection of project plans can be found in books, magazines, and through mail-order catalogs. When you add the ability to adapt different plans to your own particular tastes, you can expand your creative horizons even further.

Saving money is also an important advantage but certainly not the only one. There is a great deal of satisfaction derived from creating something with your own hands. The patience and care involved in constructing a beautiful strawberry tower, for instance, are generously rewarded in midsummer when you can stand and admire not only your craftsmanship but your green thumb as well. The gardener, who is also a woodworker, is truly twice blessed.

In an effort to create garden structures and accessories that hold their own in the company of a well-groomed flower or vegetable garden, we set about designing and building 18 projects that will add charm and elegance to any landscape. This book is a collection of these projects. They are relatively easy to build and aesthetically designed with traditional details. Their sturdy construction will give years of service while evoking the charm of bygone days. Clear, step-by-step instructions, along with numerous measured drawings and photographs, guide you through every project.

Whether you choose to build a potting bench, a plant stand, or a greenhouse, take your garden a step beyond the normal fare with *Classic Garden Structures*.

1

Tools and Materials

Those of us drawn by the beauty and tran-
quility that comes from gardening inevitably
face the desire to add accessories to the garden.
Some are practical, such as potting benches and
cold frames, while others are sought for the
aesthetic beauty they bring to the landscape,
such as obelisks and trellises. Even simple structures purchased from garden centers or hardware
stores can be very expensive, while the selection
is often limited. Because of this, the lure of
home-built outdoor accessories has always
been present.

But before we begin with the projects in this book, a brief discussion of tools and materials may be helpful. While a well-equipped woodshop is certainly the dream of every serious woodworker, most of the projects in this book can be done with a basic complement of hand and power tools. Wherever possible, we have tried to make use of common materials in standard sizes to avoid an excessive amount of cutting and waste. The finishes applied to these projects will help ensure many years of service in and around the garden with a minimum of maintenance.

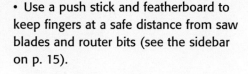

Safety Tips

Safety should be the number-one priority when working with tools and power equipment.

• Always wear safety glasses when working with power tools.

• Follow manufacturers' directions when using any tools.

• Never remove or defeat the proper operation of safety guards on all power equipment.

• Use a push stick and featherboard to keep fingers at a safe distance from saw blades and router bits (see the sidebar on p. 15).

• Avoid distractions when working with power equipment: Your best defense against injury is your total concentration on the work you're doing.

• Apply paints and other finishes outside or in a well-ventilated area.

• Wear a face mask to protect yourself from sawdust and other suspended particles in the workplace.

• Wear hearing protectors (earplugs or earmuffs) when operating loud machinery.

• Wear a dual-cartridge respirator to protect yourself from the harmful fumes of paints, lacquers, and solvents.

A collection of hand saws (clockwise from top): crosscut saw, backsaw, hacksaw, and coping saw.

TOOLS

Having the right tool always makes your job faster and easier. Fortunately, you don't need an elaborate set of tools to accomplish most of the projects presented in this book, only a basic assortment of hand and power tools. If you don't have a good complement of hand tools, consider purchasing basic starter sets from a quality manufacturer. You can generally get a much better price buying in sets, rather than buying tools individually.

HAND SAWS

If you had to choose just one saw for your toolbox, a crosscut saw would be the logical choice. It typically has between 6 teeth per inch (tpi) and 12 tpi (more teeth produce a finer cut) and is a favorite as an all–around saw. However, it was specifically designed to cut across the grain of the wood.

A backsaw is generally used for making precise cuts. Its thin blade is kept rigid by a reinforcing strip of metal along its top edge. The length of the blade is usually no more than 15 in. and has between 12 tpi and 15 tpi. This is a

An assortment of hammers (clockwise): rubber mallet, 13-ounce claw hammer, 16-ounce claw hammer with cast handle, and 20-ounce claw hammer with fiberglass handle.

A selection of chisels and screwdrivers (clockwise): wood chisel set, Phillips-tip screwdriver set, square-tip screwdriver, and straight-tip screwdriver set.

great saw for mitering moldings when used in conjunction with a miter box.

A coping saw has a thin, 6-in. blade held under tension by a U-shaped metal frame. The blade allows you to cut a much tighter arc than with other saws and is often used for cutting curves and intricate shapes.

A hacksaw is mostly used for cutting metal but works equally well on certain plastics, such as PVC pipe. There are several types of hacksaw blades available. Generally, blades with fewer teeth are used to cut hard metals, while blades with more teeth are used to cut softer metals. As with most saw blades, choosing a middle ground with respect to the number of teeth per inch will usually suffice for most projects.

HAMMERS

At most hardware stores, you will find a large assortment of hammers from which to choose. Like most tools, hammers are often designed to fill a particular niche, such as a framer's hammer or a tack hammer. But for most people, a basic claw hammer is a good place to start. Because you can use one hammer to accomplish most of your building tasks, make sure you purchase the best quality you can afford.

Hammers come in different weights, generally between 13 ounces and 20 ounces. You may eventually want to have two or three hammers of different weights, but a 16-ounce one is probably the best choice for the first hammer you buy. A heavier hammer makes it easier to drive large nails, however, your arm may tire quickly. One other important consideration is the handle construction. After breaking several wooden handles (usually made from hickory), we now prefer a metal hammer that is cast in one piece. The new fiberglass handles are also very tough and may be another good choice.

A mallet, which is closely related to a hammer, is a great tool to have in your toolbox. Either a rubber or wooden one will safely drive a wood chisel (which usually has a plastic or wooden handle) or nudge a piece of finished lumber into position without marring the surface.

SCREWDRIVERS AND CHISELS

There are two basic types of screw-drivers that should be part of every toolbox: a straight tip and a Phillips tip (crosshead). A third choice is a square-tip screwdriver that drives a matching square-head screw. While not as common as the other two, this type of fastener is quickly gaining popularity with serious woodworkers because of its positive grab.

The most important consideration when using any type of screwdriver is how well the tip of the screwdriver matches the head of the screw. Using the appropriate tip will avoid damage to the surrounding wood as well as damage to the screw head. For this reason, an assortment of good screwdrivers is nec-essary to properly drive various screw sizes. Here again, the most economical way to obtain a good variety of screw-drivers is to buy a packaged set.

An array of wood chisels is practical to have on hand. These often come in sets of four ranging in size from ¼ in. to 1 in. Wood chisels have a number of uses including the creation of notches, mortises, and tenons. Always drive a chisel with a rubber or wooden mallet and keep the blades sharpened with a sharpening stone. Since chisels need to remain very sharp to work properly, it's important to store them separately from

your other tools. Doing this will also prevent accidental cuts while searching for a chisel in a crowded toolbox.

WRENCHES AND PLIERS

Most outdoor projects use fasteners such as nails and wood screws, but on occasion the use of nuts, bolts, and lag screws will make a set of wrenches a must. The most common wrench is the combination wrench, which has an open-ended wrench on one side and a box wrench on the other. An adjustable

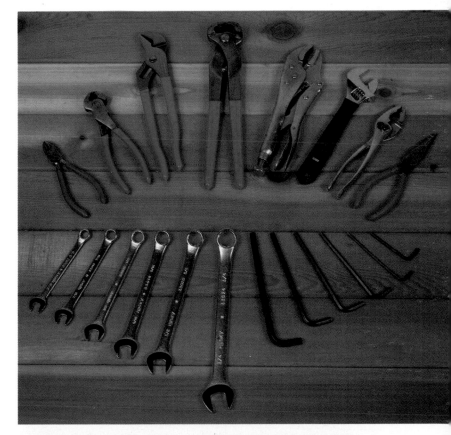

A collection of wrenches, pliers, and nippers (clockwise from top center): nail nippers, locking pliers, adjustable wrench, slip-joint pliers, needle-nose pliers, hex wrench set, combination wrench set, diagonal-cutting pliers, small nail nippers, and tongue-and-groove pliers.

wrench; as the name implies, can adjust to a variety of sizes and can help fill the gap for any missing combination–wrench sizes.

In addition, wrenches are a necessity for adjusting power equipment. Belts need tightening, blades need changing, and tables need leveling. This type of work also may require a set of hex wrenches (sometimes known as Allen wrenches). These L-shaped hexagonal bars work in much the same way as a square-tipped screwdriver and

usually come packaged in a wide variety of sizes.

A good assortment of pliers is another important component of a well-stocked toolbox. Besides having a pair of standard slip–joint pliers, you might consider adding a pair of locking pliers, needle–nose pliers, and possibly a pair of diagonal cutters or nail nippers for cutting wire.

CLAMPS

All clamps are basically designed to do just one job: hold things together. The reasons might be to glue two or more boards together or simply to hold material in place until they can be secured with nails or screws. Clamps come in many styles including C-clamps, bar clamps, spring clamps, and miter clamps. The newest type of clamp is an innovative, lightweight bar clamp featuring a quick–release pistol grip. It is easily locked into position by using only one hand, which is a big advantage when you're working by yourself.

LEVELS, SQUARES, AND TAPE MEASURES

Building permanent structures, such as arbors, sheds, fences, and walls, requires the use of one or more spirit levels. A 12–in. level, for example, is adequate for small jobs, such as leveling a shelf. Longer levels are best for leveling concrete block and wood framing. A 3–ft. to 4–ft. level, made of wood or aluminum, is a good choice for most outdoor projects.

For checking two points several feet apart, use an inexpensive string level. This small, lightweight spirit level relies on a taut string for an accurate mea–

A variety of clamps (from top left to right): pipe clamp, spring clamp, C-clamp, miter clamp, quick-release bar clamp, quick-release bar clamp with pistol grip, and hand-screw clamp.

surement. For greater distances, a water level is a better choice. It uses two clear plastic tubes attached to either end of a garden hose. When filled with water, it accurately checks the level of materials at distances limited only by the length of your hose.

To construct most outdoor projects, you will need some type of square. A carpenter's square is generally used for laying out rafters and squaring boards. The smaller combination square has a built-in spirit level and is handy for marking 90° or 45° angles. An adjustable protractor is another good measuring tool. It can be locked to any angle setting and doubles as a circular saw guide.

A 25-ft. steel measuring tape is another essential tool for any work site. While it is flexible, the tape is also cupped to help prevent it from bending when extended. The only drawback to a steel tape is that it can be easily damaged, so it should always be retracted immediately after measuring.

For measuring greater distances, our favorite is a 100-ft. fiberglass reel tape. It's perfect for squaring up foundations or laying out garden beds. And, because it's not a steel tape, it won't rust or easily break.

CIRCULAR SAW

A portable electric circular saw is probably the most used power tool that we own. Even if you have a table saw, it's impractical to continually carry lumber and plywood back and forth from the yard to the shop for cutting. With a circular saw, you can cut, rip, and miter boards to length, all on the job site. Circular saws come in several sizes, however, the most common takes a 7¼-in. blade.

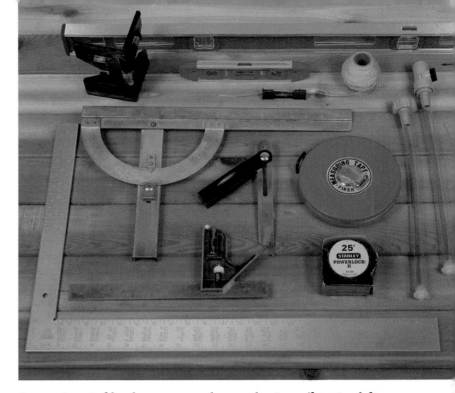

An assortment of levels, squares, and measuring tapes (from top left to right): 4-ft. carpenter's level, post level, torpedo level, line level, water level, framing square, adjustable protractor and saw blade, bevel gauge, 100-ft. fiberglass reel tape, combination square, and 25-ft. steel measuring rule.

A circular saw.

When a circular saw is used in conjunction with a straightedge or adjustable protractor, you'll be surprised at how straight and accurate your cuts can be. It's also helpful to have a couple of sturdy sawhorses so you can work at a comfortable height.

As with all power tools, it's important to wear safety glasses when working with a circular saw. It's also important to use a heavy–duty outdoor extension cord and to be aware of the cord's location while you're cutting. When used properly, a circular saw will enable you to construct many outdoor projects.

DRILLS

If we were to rank power tools in order of their importance, a ⅜–in. variable-speed, reversing drill would be a close second to a circular saw. Besides doing the obvious job of drilling clearance holes for bolts or pilot holes for screws, a drill can be used to drive in any type of screw with the right type of driver bit. This can save a lot of wear and tear on your wrists. The reverse setting lets you extract screws with the same amount of ease.

A variety of drills (clockwise): cordless drill, drill, and hand brace.

A sabersaw.

In recent years, portable electric drills have improved in two important ways. First, many now come with keyless chucks, making it easier and faster to change bits. Second, there are many cordless models that finally free you from the tether of a power cord. These improvements make this important tool even more desirable.

A traditional hand brace still has a place in a modern toolbox. The slow and deliberate pace of the brace and bit can help to drill an accurate hole at a precise depth. It is also handy on job sites where power is not available.

SABERSAW

Many outdoor projects can be made using only three power tools: a circular saw, a drill, and a sabersaw. A sabersaw excels at cutting contours, curves, and circle cutouts. We used a sabersaw to cut out the half–circle shelves of the Potted Plant Stand (see pp. 78–83). There are blades available that will cut easily through most materials, including wood, plastic, and even thin sheet metal. To get the best cut from a sabersaw, use a sharp blade and avoid pushing the saw through the material being cut. Too much force or a dull blade can cause the blade to wander, bend, or in some cases break. Most sabersaws also allow you to tilt the blade up to 45°, a feature that came in handy when we needed to chamfer the edges of the Strawberry Tower center post (see pp. 112–117).

ROUTER

Over time, adding specialized tools to your workshop can greatly expand your creative options. A portable router is a wonderful tool for applying decorative edges to wood and adds a professional look to the finished project. Besides cutting decorative edges, there are router bits for cutting dadoes, rabbets, slots, and dovetail joints.

There are two basic types of routers: a fixed router and a plunge router. A fixed router is lowered onto, or moved into, the material you are cutting. A plunge router allows you to rest the router base on the material's surface and then plunge the bit into contact with the wood by moving the motor housing along spring–loaded columns. For most projects, a moderately priced fixed router is sufficient.

A router.

TABLE SAW

A table saw usually becomes the hub of most woodshops. It normally consists of a 10-in. blade protruding up through a large metal table equipped with a miter gauge and rip fence. The bread-and-butter use of the table saw is for cutting boards and sheet stock to size. However, it is also excellent for cutting dadoes,

A table saw.

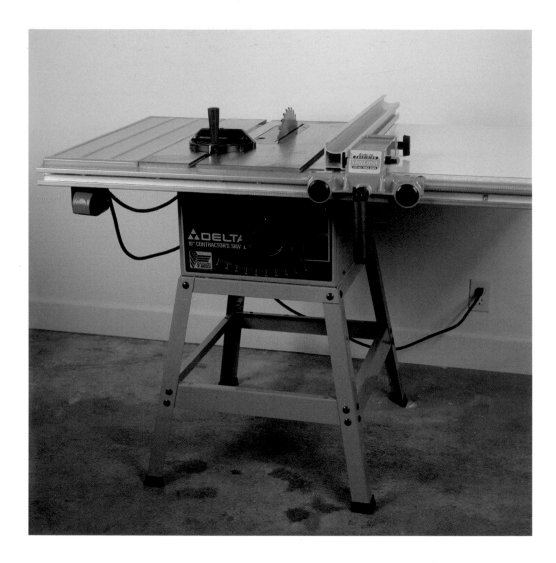

slots, rabbets, tenons, and miters. To further increase its productivity, a wide variety of jigs and accessories are available. We used the miter gauge along with a tapering jig to make the finials used in the Pole Bean Trellis (see pp. 40–42) and at the two ends of the Greenhouse roof (see pp. 137–139).

A table saw is a powerful tool but also a hazardous one. It's very important to follow all of the recommended safety instructions when working with any piece of shop equipment. In addition, when operating a table saw, use a push stick, featherboard, and other types of jigs to make your job easier and safer.

Push Stick and Featherboard

A featherboard and push stick in use.

Push stick and featherboard patterns

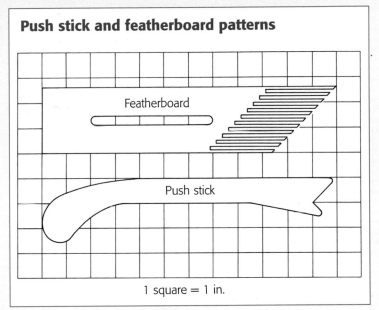

Featherboard

Push stick

1 square = 1 in.

A push stick and featherboard are two important safety accessories to have in any home shop setting. The purpose of a push stick is to keep your fingers away from the high-speed blades of table saws, routers, and other shop equipment. A featherboard is generally used on table saws and table-mounted routers. It holds a piece of wood firmly against the guide or rip fence while the stock is fed through the blade. This helps to keep the blade from binding and produces a straight cut. It also eliminates the temptation to use your fingers to achieve the same result.

While these two shop accessories are inexpensive and can be purchased through most woodworking catalogs, they are also very easy to make. Using the grid patterns at top right, transfer the push stick or featherboard outline to a ¾-in.-thick piece of clear wood (a hardwood such as oak is a good choice). Cut out the shape of the push stick with a coping saw or sabersaw, then sand the edges smooth. The featherboard is best cut to size on a table saw. Use a saw blade with a kerf (the saw-blade cut) that is approximately ⅛ in. to

Featherboard assembly

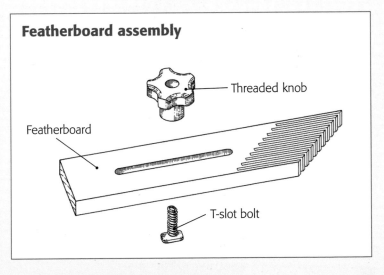

Threaded knob

Featherboard

T-slot bolt

create the set of "feathers" on one end of the board. Drill two ⅜-in. holes at each end of the center slot, then remove the wood in between with a coping saw (see the illustration above). Use a tightening knob and T-slot bolt to clamp the featherboard to the saw table.

An assortment of woods suitable for outdoor projects (from left to right): pine, hemlock, poplar, oak, cedar, redwood, pressure-treated wood (rated for aboveground use), and pressure-treated wood (rated for belowground use).

WOODS

Selecting the right wood to use for a particular outdoor project can be a confusing process, especially since there are a wide variety of woods from which to choose. The best way to approach this decision is to answer a few fundamental questions about the project you have in mind, such as your budget, the types of woods available in your area, how much weather the project will be exposed to, and whether it will be totally aboveground or sit partially belowground.

Most woods are classified into two basic categories: hardwoods and softwoods. Hardwoods come from broadleafed trees and include such familiar woods as oak, maple, birch, and poplar.

Softwoods come from coniferous trees and include wood varieties such as cedar, redwood, fir, spruce, and hemlock. While hardwoods may be appropriate for some outdoor projects, especially where additional strength may be needed, most outdoor projects are generally constructed from one or more softwoods.

We designed most of the projects in this book to take advantage of standard sizes and readily available materials. If some woods given in the materials lists are not available in your area, you may need to substitute different woods with similar characteristics. Many lumberyards and home centers will let you choose your own wood. This is a real advantage because you can select the best. Look for boards that are straight, have few knots, and have been stored out of the weather. If you can't choose your own wood, only deal with a lumberyard that you trust; it's frustrating to work with lumber that is warped or misshapen. Choosing good-quality lumber that is right for the job will make your final garden project both durable and attractive.

COST

When choosing a wood, price is often an overriding consideration. While you will save a great deal of money by providing "sweat equity," the choice of wood also can make a big difference in the final cost. For instance, teak is undoubtedly one of the most weather-resistant woods you can purchase, but at a cost of several times that of western red cedar it probably won't fit into most people's budgets.

The grade of wood is another factor that can have a big influence on the cost of a project. Clear woods, which are devoid of knots, will have a much higher cost than woods containing some knots and imperfections. If you intend to apply a clear preservative finish to your project so that the natural grain and color of the wood will show, then a clear grade of wood might be desirable. But if you intend to apply a semitransparent stain, opaque stain, or exterior paint, a #2 or "tight-knot" grade might be perfectly adequate.

AVAILABILITY

The area in which you live will have an influence on the available selection of woods as well as on the cost. In our area of western Washington, western red cedar is moderately priced and readily available. The same is true for Douglas fir, since both of these trees are harvested in the northwest. Redwood, on the other hand, is much harder to find even though it comes from nearby California and Oregon. On the East Coast, pine and white cedar are common and will generally be more moderately priced.

WEATHER EXPOSURE

The amount of weather your project will be subjected to is another important consideration when selecting wood to use outdoors. The type of wood, coupled with the type of protective finish you apply (see Finishes on pp. 20–21), will determine how many years you can enjoy your handiwork. Cedar and redwood are good choices for outdoor projects because they contain natural oils and resins that inhibit decay and resist damage from insects. These woods work well for garden trellises, arbors, fences, raised beds, and greenhouses. Fir, pine, hemlock, poplar, and spruce work

nicely for accessories that can be stored in bad weather, such as garden sieves, row markers, plant stands, dibbles, and plant caddies. They also work well for structures that don't come in direct contact with the ground.

ABOVEGROUND OR BELOWGROUND

For projects that will be partially buried in the ground, it's imperative to use a wood that is resistant to decay, such as cedar, redwood, or pressure-treated wood. The constant contact with microorganisms and moisture in the soil will cause buried wood to deteriorate much more rapidly than wood sitting aboveground. While there has been much controversy about the use of pressure-treated wood, especially in a garden setting, it nonetheless has become the predominant material used for outdoor structures. The reason is simply cost and availability. Several different types of softwoods can be pressure treated, which results in low prices and a ready supply in most areas.

The controversy stems from the chemicals used to treat the wood and whether or not these chemicals can leach into the soil. While there has been no hard evidence that we have seen to support the idea that leaching is a problem, we have decided to use pressure-treated wood only in projects that aren't in direct contact with food crops. For instance, we used cedar boards for the sides of our raised beds but used pressure-treated posts at either end of our berry trellises where the plants were at least 3 ft. away. Ultimately, gardeners will have to make up their own minds whether or not to use pressure-treated wood based on the results of ongoing research.

FASTENERS

After you decide what type of wood to use for a particular project, you need to decide what type of fasteners will hold the various pieces together. Today, there is a wide assortment of nails, screws, and specialized fasteners using a variety of weather-resistant coatings and compositions. A brief look at some of the fasteners that are available may help you make the right choice for the job.

NAILS

While there are many types of nails, most outdoor construction will use either common box nails or finishing nails. Nail sizes are designated by a small "d" following the number, which is the "penny" size. This is a throwback to England when 100 nails were sold for a certain number of pennies. The most commonly used sizes are between 4d (1½ in.) and 16d (3½ in.). Box nails are most often used for rough framing and have a flat head, which makes the nail easy to remove. Finishing nails have a small, slightly flared head, which is ideal for moldings and small trim.

Moisture corrosion is your number-one concern when choosing nails for use outdoors. Fortunately, there are several types of nails made specifically for this purpose. Hot-dipped galvanized nails have a relatively thick coating of zinc and provide good corrosion resistance. The one problem with galvanized nails is that they tend to leave a black stain around the nail head when used on redwood and cedar, which is due to the tannic acid in the wood. This is only a problem if you will be protecting the wood with a clear waterproofing sealer. If you plan to cover the wood with

primer and paint, it won't be a concern. If you are going to put a natural finish on the wood, try to locate either stainless steel or aluminum nails, which won't rust or cause stains.

SCREWS

For most of our garden projects, our fastener of choice is the screw. Screws securely lock wood pieces together and won't back out, as nails sometimes do over time. They also give you the option of disassembling the project in the event you want to move or store it.

The designation of screw sizes is made up of two parts. For instance, if you see #8 x 2½ on the package, the first number is the gauge or size of the shank, while the second number refers to the length in inches. Wood screws usually come in one of three head shapes: flat, oval, and round. For most woodworking projects, you will probably use the flat head, which will be countersunk below the surface of the wood. You will also need to decide on one of three types of screwdriver heads: the standard slotted head, Phillips head, and square-drive head. The square-drive head is our favorite because it doesn't "cam-out" or strip as easily as the others do. The Phillips head is a good second choice.

Corrosion resistance is as important with screws as it is with other types of fasteners. Wood screws come in a variety of finishes, colors, and compositions to match the needs of almost any situation. Starting with the least weather-resistant, some of the screws available for outdoor use are yellow zinc, galvanized, galvanized with a polymer coating, brass, stainless steel, and silicon bronze. Sometimes the choice between two corrosion-resistant screws is more a

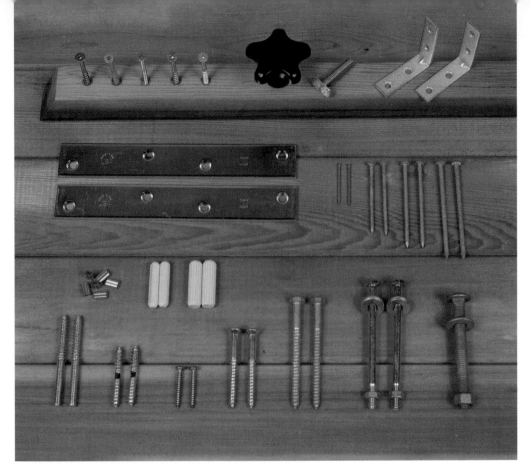

Commonly used outdoor fasteners (from left to right): yellow zinc, galvanized, brass, stainless steel, and silicon bronze screws, five-star knob, T-slot bolt, galvanized corner braces, galvanized mending plates, galvanized 4d finishing nails, galvanized 8d box nails, galvanized 10d box nails, galvanized 16d box nails, cable ferrules, hardwood dowels, galvanized hanger bolts, galvanized dowel screws, stainless steel round-head screws, galvanized flat-head wood screws, galvanized lag bolts, galvanized hex-head bolts, and galvanized carriage bolts.

matter of appearance than anything else. This might be the case when choosing between the cool gray color of stainless steel screws and the warm brassy–yellow color of silicon bronze screws.

DOWELS AND OTHER FASTENERS

Wood dowels are another type of fastener that deserves mention. Many projects in this book, including the Strawberry Tower, Cold Frame, and Greenhouse windows, use hardwood dowels to join pieces together. These

joints are very strong and will hold up for years. A doweling jig makes the job of aligning the matching drill holes painless and accurate (see the sidebar on p. 63). We have also used the jig for drilling straight pilot holes for other types of fasteners, such as dowel screws and hanger bolts. The jig accepts several bit sizes to accommodate an assortment of dowel sizes.

Wooden biscuits are another good method of joining wood edge to edge. However, this method requires a biscuit cutter, which is a bit more expensive than a doweling jig.

In addition to the types of fasteners already mentioned, there are many other fasteners you may have use for when working on a project. Part of the fun in building a new structure lies in the exploration of area hardware stores. For the projects in this book, other types of fasteners we have used include hanger bolts, dowel screws, mending plates, angle brackets, cable ferrules, lag screws, and carriage bolts. Most of these items will come in a corrosion-resistant version, whether it's galvanized, stainless steel, or brass. Always choose this level of protection for all fasteners to help prolong the life of your outdoor projects and accessories.

FINISHES

Once the pieces of your project are cut out and fastened together, you can step back and admire the fruits of your labor. Unfortunately, the time spent gazing with pride at your handiwork will soon come under pressure with the sight of gathering rain clouds on the horizon. Your work is not yet done. To finish the job, you need to protect your project from the inevitable onslaught of nasty weather.

While there are many ways to finish an outdoor woodworking project, your choices will basically fall into one of three categories: clear finishes, stains, and paints.

Hardware stores and home centers provide an amazing array of products from which to choose. The difficulty comes in deciding not only what type of finish to select but also what color. Ultimately, choosing color is subjective and there are few wrong decisions. It usually comes down to which finish will best blend with the rest of your garden.

CLEAR FINISHES

Clear finishes let the natural color of the wood show through and are often made of highly refined linseed oil. Their main purpose is to seal and waterproof, however, some manufacturers are also adding mildewcides and UV inhibitors. These additives help prevent mold, mildew, fungus, and natural graying of the wood. If you prefer your project to gray over time, look for a finish that does not include UV inhibitors.

Some clear waterproofing sealers specify that they can be covered with a paint or stain once they are dry. This provides a good opportunity for adding double protection to your project, especially when protecting woods other than cedar and redwood. This method has worked well on many of our projects.

STAINS

Transparent stains add a color tint to wood without hiding the grain. Similar in makeup to waterproofing sealers, they are often used to enhance the color of wood or to mimic another species. For instance, you might apply a transparent redwood finish to cedar or fir. This can give you the look of a more expensive wood without the cost.

Semitransparent stains have a higher concentration of pigments than transparent stains but still let some of the natural wood grain show through. Having some pigment in the stain is helpful when there are several different shades of wood in your project. Once applied, semitransparent stains tend to even out the differences in shades, producing a much more pleasing effect. The cedar tongue-and-groove siding we used for the Vegetable Washstand ranged from a light blonde to a rusty brown. The final result shown on p. 84 has a nice even finish.

Solid-color stains (sometimes referred to as opaque stains) contain the most pigment and in appearance resemble oil or latex paint. However, they still allow the natural texture of the wood to remain. We used an oil/latex combination on several of our projects, including the Pole Bean Trellis and the Planter Box and Obelisk. After drying for a few days, these stains exhibited excellent adhesion and durability.

PAINTS

Standard exterior oil or latex paint remains the most familiar finish for outdoor projects. The Berry Trellis and most of our garden fencing is covered with a good-quality exterior latex paint. This choice of finish has held up well, even through our soggy western Washington winters. But before you paint over bare wood, always prepare it first with a coat of an oil-based primer/sealer. This will give the paint a good surface to adhere to, as well as sealing in any sap or oils in the wood. Using the primer/sealer combination is especially important when preparing redwood or cedar for painting. Even with the sealer applied, you may still find a little of the brownish oils seeping to the surface. If this does happen, just wipe it off with a damp rag after the paint has dried.

No matter what type of finish you choose, always purchase the best quality

you can afford. The higher-priced finishes can actually work out to be more economical if they last for a longer period of time. It's also important to read all of the label information before purchasing a particular finish to ensure that it is right for your project. Many finishes and waterproofing sealers are nontoxic once they are dry, so they can be used in vegetable gardens. With the right finish, you can enjoy the garden structure you've built without a second thought about impending bad weather.

Finishes for outdoor projects (from left to right): no finish, waterproofing sealer, transparent stain, semitransparent stain, solid-color stain, and oil-based primer with exterior latex paint.

2

Trellises and Plant Supports

The heritage of trellises and plant supports is one of simple practicality. They supply vertical growing space that conserves precious room in garden beds, they keep ripening fruits and vegetables well above the damp earth, and they provide proper support to plant varieties that need routine pruning and training. But these useful structures can also bring visual interest to your landscape. The following projects, the Tomato Trellis, Berry Trellis, Pole Bean Trellis, and Planter Box and Obelisk, are all designed to bring classical elegance to your garden while offering years of support to your vines.

TOMATO TRELLIS

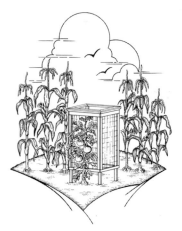

The wire-frame tomato cages sold at local garden centers are inexpensive and easy to use. Simply plunge the pronged end of the frame into the soil and you're ready for tomato season. But the aesthetically minded kitchen gardener might prefer a tomato trellis that not only supports the vines but also contributes architectural interest to the vegetable garden.

This classic trellis does both. It offers 8 linear ft. of growing area, while having a footprint of only 4 sq. ft. Add to this a trim of cove molding and simple, sturdy construction, and the result is a welcome addition to the garden that will last for years. The trellis can be used to support a variety of vines including cucumbers, peas, and sweet peas.

When preparing materials, you may want to wait until it's time to install the cove molding before mitering so you can place the pieces on the frame and mark them for an exact fit.

Sturdy construction and architectural styling make this Tomato Trellis a welcome addition to any kitchen garden.

TOMATO TRELLIS MATERIALS LIST

Key	Qty.	Description	Finished Dimensions	Material
A	4	Trellis legs	1½ in. x 1½ in. x 48 in.	Cedar
B	4	Side frame pieces	¾ in. x 1½ in. x 34½ in.	Cedar
C	2	Bottom frame pieces	¾ in. x 1½ in. x 21½ in.	Cedar
D	2	Top frame pieces	¾ in. x 2⅝ in. x 21½ in.	Cedar
E	4	Side frame pieces	¾ in. x 2¼ in. x 34½ in.	Cedar
F	2	Bottom frame pieces	¾ in. x 1½ in. x 23 in.	Cedar
G	2	Top frame pieces	¾ in. x 2⅝ in. x 23 in.	Cedar
H	4	Top cap trim	¾ in. x 3½ in. x 25½ in.	Cedar
I	4	Top cove moldings	1⅛ in. x 25¼ in.	Pine or fir
J	4	Wire fence panels	20 in. x 36 in. (2-in. x 4-in. weld)	Galvanized
K	80	Wire fence staples	½ in. to ¾ in.	Galvanized
L	48	Outdoor screws	#8 x 1½ in.	Galvanized or stainless steel
M	24	Finishing nails	4d	Galvanized

1 Make two opposing frames by assembling cedar boards (A, B, C, D) with screws (L), as shown in the top left illustration on the facing page.

2 Connect these two frames using cedar boards (E, F, G), as shown in the top right illustration on the facing page. While securing these boards in place, keep the resulting frame as square as possible. When you're finished, you will have the basic frame of the trellis completed.

3 Stand the frame up on a solid, flat surface and set the four mitered boards (H) on top of the frame (see the bottom illustration on the facing page). Before installing them, make sure the trellis

frame is square and all the mitered corners match. Then secure the four top boards (H) with two screws (L) per side along the top edges of boards (D, G) as well as the top ends of boards (A). Installing the four top boards will keep the entire frame square.

4 Cut your cove molding (I) into four pieces approximately 30 in. long. Make a 45° miter at one end of your first piece, then pencil mark the exact point on the molding for your second miter after placing the molding under the lip of board (H) and next to boards (D) or (G), as shown in the detail profile at right on p. 28. When mitering crown or cove moldings, the piece of molding must be held at the same orientation as it will be

Constructing the opposing frames

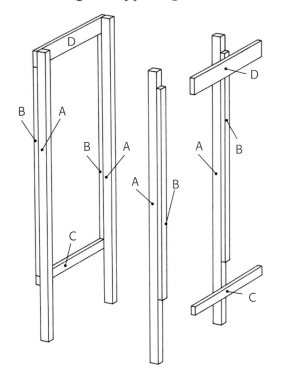

Connecting the opposing frames

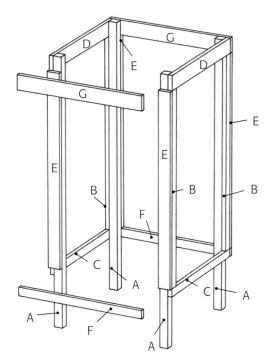

Installing the top boards

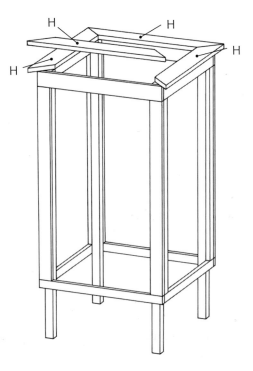

installed, in other words, at a 45° angle to the base of the miter box or saw table (see the sidebar on cutting molding on pp. 30–31). Secure the molding to the frame with finishing nails (M), pre-drilling to prevent the wood from split-ting. Repeat this step to install the re-maining three sections of cove molding.

5 After the trellis frame is assembled, apply a finish. We applied two coats of a clear, paintable waterproofing sealer to help extend the life of the trellis. After the waterproofing sealer was dry, we applied a rich green opaque stain, which helped the trellis blend into our overall garden setting.

6 After the final finish is dry, attach the four wire fence panels (J) that will support the plants (see the illustration at

Neatly mitered mold-ings add a classic finish-ing touch to this trellis.

Attaching the wire fence panels

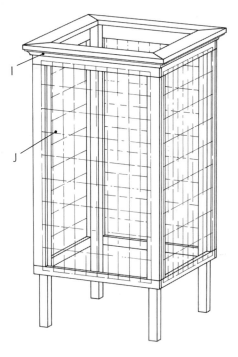

Inset of top board and molding assembly

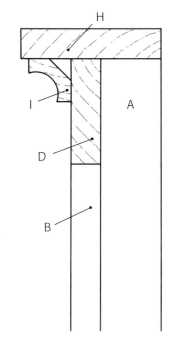

left on the facing page). To make the panels easier to attach to the frame, take some of the curl out of each section of fence before attempting to fasten it. Secure each piece of fencing to the frame with 20 fence staples (K) per side. The fencing will overlap the frame approximately ¾ in. on all sides.

7 Once the fence panels are securely in place, decide where to locate the trellis in your garden. Before installation, prepare and amend the soil as you normally would in your vegetable garden. Set the trellis frame in place and lightly push down on the top just enough to leave a set of four leg impressions, then set the trellis aside. Using a scrap piece of 2x2 and a mallet, create four holes about 5 in. to 6 in. deep that match the location of the four legs. Then set the trellis frame in place and lightly push the legs into the holes. Creating the leg holes first with a scrap piece of wood avoids unnecessary torque on the frame.

As your plants grow, they can be secured to the trellis fencing with small twist-ties. Be sure to keep the ties rather loose to avoid damaging the plant stems. In a few weeks, your trellis will reward your efforts by hosting an abundant harvest.

Create holes for the trellis legs by pounding a stake into the soil.

This trellis can easily support four large tomato plants.

Cutting Molding

The cove molding used in the Tomato Trellis, as well as many other types of moldings, can be mitered with a simple miter box and backsaw. When positioning the piece of molding in the miter box, it's important to orient it in the same way it sits against the top cap piece (H) and the top frame piece (D) of the Tomato Trellis. The base of the miter box would be equivalent to the top cap piece, and the sidewall of the box would equal the top frame piece. Cut the first miter with the saw in one of the 45° slots, as shown in the photo below.

To cut the matching piece of molding for each corner, simply move the backsaw to the opposite 45° slot in the miter box. For this cut, the molding is fed into the box from the opposite end (see the top photo on the facing page). Alternately, you can cut corner miters on a table saw in much the same way, except you would be moving the molding through the saw blade instead of the reverse. With the miter gauge set at 45°, hold the molding against the gauge as if it were the sidewall of the miter box. The saw table would be equivalent to the base of the miter box. For the matching piece, just slip the miter gauge rail into the guide slot on the opposite side of the blade and set the opposing 45° angle on the gauge.

If your pieces were properly positioned when cut, they should match up to form a

Cut the first miter using a backsaw in one of the 45° slots.

clean 90° corner, as shown in the bottom photo. It's helpful to start with an oversized piece of molding and trim it to size. For the Tomato Trellis, we made our first miter cut on each piece of molding, then placed it up against the frame so we could pencil mark the exact point at which to cut the other side. By following these simple instructions, you should have no problem adding that extra touch of detail offered by decorative moldings.

Cut the matching piece of molding using the opposite 45° slot.

Both mitered pieces should match up to form a 90° corner.

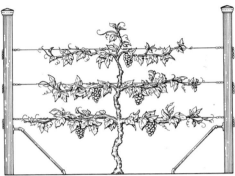

A system of posts and wires is the tradi–
tional method for supporting cane fruits
and fruiting vines. Without proper
pruning and support, cane fruits such as
raspberries, blackberries, and tayberries
will quickly become brier patches, and
fruiting vines such as grapes will grow
into tangled, dense thickets. Berry
trellises can be made in many ways
from a variety of materials, but we feel
the sleek and sturdy design of this Berry
Trellis will keep your soft fruits neatly
trained while adding a touch of elegance
to your kitchen garden.

The decorative, capped end posts,
together with the wires and pipe sup–
ports, make this project a perfect blend
of form and function. The trellis derives
its strength from the iron pipe supports,
yet the pipes' slim diameter keeps them
unobtrusive. And it's easy to maintain
the trellis's trim and taught appearance
by simply adjusting the chains that are
attached to the wire ends. This project is

**Support your
berry canes
and fruit-
bearing vines
with this dec-
orative yet
sturdy trellis.**

BERRY TRELLIS MATERIALS LIST

Key	Qty.	Description	Finished Dimensions	Material
A	2	End posts	3½ in. x 3½ in. x 108 in.	Cedar or treated
B	2	Fence caps	To fit 3½-in. x 3½-in. post	Cedar
C	2	Floor flanges	3½ in. dia. for ½-in. pipe	Galvanized
D	2	Pipes	½ in. x 2 in.	Galvanized
E	2	Pipes	½ in. x 24 in.	Galvanized
F	2	Pipes	½ in. x 6 in.	Galvanized
G	4	45° elbow fittings	½ in.	Galvanized
H	2	End caps	½ in.	Galvanized
I	8	Screws	#14 x 2½ in.	Galvanized
J	4	Concrete	60-lb. bag (½ cu. ft.)	Premix concrete
K	6	Single jack chains	#12 x 12 in.	Galvanized
L	6	Tension rods	⅛ in. x 3 in.	Brass or aluminum
M	3	Trellis support wires	14 gauge x 20 ft.	Galvanized or aluminum
N	6	Cable ferrules	12 gauge to 14 gauge	Aluminum

easy to build with all the required mate-rials readily available at your local home and hardware center.

Before starting work on the Berry Trellis, lay out the bed and prepare the soil as you would for any garden space.

1 At your chosen site, measure off the location of each end post. You can vary the distance between the end posts to fit your needs, but if you try to span a distance greater than 20 ft. you may need to install a middle post to support the wires (see the sidebar on p. 37).

2 Dig two post holes 36 in. deep where your two end posts (A) will stand. Set your first post into the hole, then use a post level or standard straight level to make sure the post is plumb. Fill the hole to within 12 in. of the surface with some of the dirt that was excavated earlier for the posthole. Continue to check your level as you tamp the dirt firm, then excavate an additional 5 in. or 6 in. out from the post.

3 Repeat the same procedure to install the second post at the opposite end of your trellis. Use a water level or line level to make sure the tops of both posts are even.

4 With both posts firmly in place, mix some premix concrete (J) to pour into the enlarged holes around each post (see the illustration at top right). Each hole should take about one 60–lb. bag. Use a cement trowel (or even a garden trowel) to work the concrete evenly around the post. Before continuing, allow the concrete to completely set, usually two or three days.

5 Assemble the set of pipe braces (C, D, E, F, G, H), as shown in the illustration at bottom right. Make sure that all pieces are tight and in line with each other. Once you have the pipe braces assembled, you can use them to mark the ground where your next set of holes will be dug. Do this by sliding one of the braces down the inside edge of each post. The spot where the end of the brace meets the ground is where you will dig the brace hole (see the photo below). Using a posthole digger, dig a hole near each post about 24 in. deep.

Diagonal pipe supports keep the trellis plumb.

Overview of post and pipe brace assembly

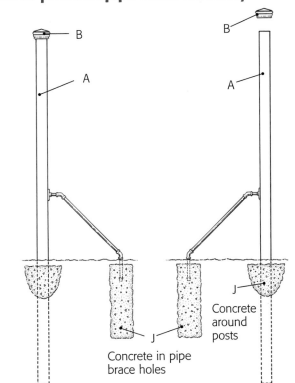

Concrete in pipe brace holes

Concrete around posts

Pipe brace assembly

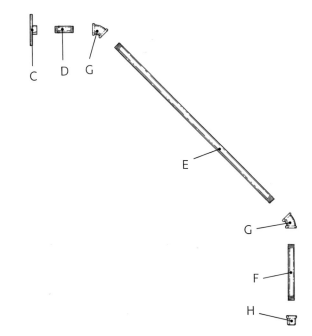

Floor flange attachment

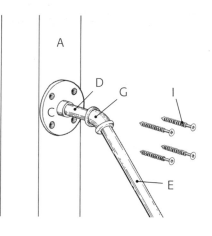

Lengths of chain and brass tension rods keep the trellis wires from sagging.

6 Before installing the pipe braces, spray them with two coats of metal primer.

7 To install the two pipe braces, measure 48 in. from the top of each post and make a pencil mark. Place the top edge of the pipe floor flange (C) at this mark. With the pipe brace in line with the center of the post and the end cap (H) at least 3 in. into the hole, pencil mark the position of the floor flange screw holes on the end post (see the illustration above).

8 Predrill the four floor flange screw holes on each post before attaching the pipe braces. With the holes drilled, mix one bag of premix concrete for each of the two brace holes. It's a good idea to have an extra bag or two of concrete handy in case you need a little more to bring the level of the concrete to the top of the hole. Fill the hole with concrete, then plunge one end of the pipe brace into the wet concrete about 3 in. to 6 in. and attach the floor flange end of the brace to the post with four screws (I). Repeat these steps for the other post.

Once again, wait two or three days for the concrete to cure before continuing work on the trellis.

9 Once the braces are attached, mark the locations for the plant support wires. While the following configuration works well for a variety of vines, you can configure your trellis in several different ways (see the sidebar on the facing page). On each post, measure 8 in. from the top and make a pencil mark in the middle of the post. Make another mark at 26 in. and a third mark at 44 in., then drill a ½-in. hole through the posts at each of these marks.

10 Before installing the wires, paint the trellis posts, caps, and braces. It's much easier to paint the posts without the wires in place.

11 To install the support wires, bend one end of each of the six tension rods (L) to a 45° angle. Next, push a 12-in. piece of chain (K) through each of the ½-in. holes until about 5 in. extends from the inside edge of the post. On the outside edge, slip a tension rod through the link closest to the post. Attach the support wire (M) to the chain using the small cable ferrules (N). Tighten the support wires by pulling the chain through the post and replacing the tension rod in a new link.

12 To complete your trellis, install the two cedar fence caps (B). These will slip easily over the top of the posts and give your berry trellis a more finished look. The caps can either be left loose or secured to the posts with 4d galvanized finishing nails. Once your trellis is finished, you are ready to plant your favorite grape or berry vines.

Adapting Your Berry Trellis

Pruning and training techniques differ with each fruit and berry variety. In fact, there can be several training techniques for a single variety. For example, grapes can be trained to a series of wires using the rod-and-spur method, the curtain method, or the Guyot or Kniffen system. There are many reference books describing these techniques (see the bibliography on p. 181), or ask your nurseryman for pruning and training advice when you buy your plants.

The illustrations at right show two ways to adapt your new post-and-wire Berry Trellis to accommodate a variety of canes and vines and their individual training needs.

Some trellising techniques require raspberries to be trained onto a series of wires positioned several feet apart. You can achieve this configuration by attaching 2x4 crossbars to the end posts (see the top illustration).

Grapevines can become very heavy, especially when they are laden with large clusters of ripe grapes. If your end posts are more than 20 ft. apart, consider installing a mid-post to keep the wires from sagging under the weight of the vines (see the bottom illustration).

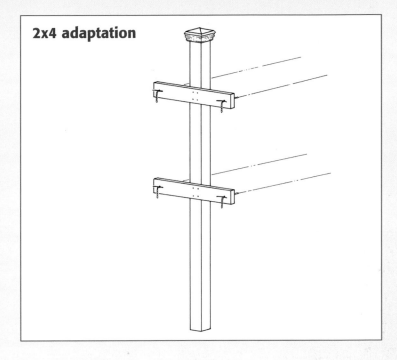

2x4 adaptation

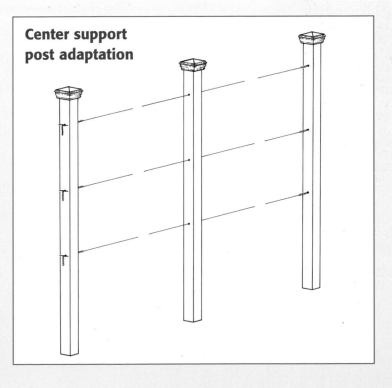

Center support post adaptation

We've all seen or constructed them at one time or another during our gardening lives: pole bean tripods made from tree limbs or scrap 2x2s, lashed together at the top with twine and placed in the garden teepee style. These trellises are immensely functional but they do little to enhance the beauty of the landscape.

Unlike its rough-and-ready counterpart, this Pole Bean Trellis has elegant lines, which make it an attractive addition to the garden. It's as comfortable in a kitchen garden supporting pole beans as it is in a formal flower garden draped in morning glories. This trellis will easily accommodate the most vigorous vines.

Standing more than 7 ft. tall, this trellis is inexpensive and easy to make. The graceful spire finial is cut from a length of 4x4 stock using a table saw and tapering jig. The same type of finial can also be adapted to other outdoor projects, including the roof ornamentation on the Greenhouse (see pp. 137–139).

This sleek and sturdy Pole Bean Trellis will elegantly support vegetable or flower vines.

POLE BEAN TRELLIS MATERIALS LIST

Key	Qty.	Description	Finished Dimensions	Material
A	1	Finial	2½ in. x 2½ in. x 22½ in.	Cedar, fir, or pine
B	4	Legs	1½ in. x 1½ in. x 82 in.	Cedar
C	4	Outdoor screws	#8 x 1½ in.	Galvanized or stainless steel
D	4	Outdoor screws	#8 x 2½ in.	Galvanized or stainless steel

1 Using a table saw, trim a 24–in. piece of 4x4 stock to 2½ in. by 2½ in. by 24 in. Then begin making the finial (A), as shown in the illustration below. Use a tapering jig to make the four 7° cuts at the top of the finial. On the top end of the finial board, use a combination square to pencil mark the center of the board by making an X from side to side (not from corner to corner). These two lines will act as a sawblade guide when starting the cut.

Using the combination square again, draw another pencil line around all four sides of the finial board about 6 in. from the opposite end. With the tapering jig set at 7° and placed against the saw fence, lay the finial board against the jig, as shown in the top left photo on the facing page. Now make a pencil mark on the tapering jig opposite the lines around the board. As you rotate the board to cut all four sides of the spire, keep these pencil lines matched up to ensure that the cuts will be even on all sides. Next, clamp the finial board to the tapering jig. Adjust the fence of the table saw so the blade starts cutting from the middle of the board, where it is marked by the X. Turn and reclamp the board three more times to complete the spire.

The next set of cuts creates the chamfered and straight dado–type grooves around the middle portion of the finial. But instead of using a dado blade, we used a standard blade and simply made several passes through the saw for each groove. To make the chamfered groove, set the sawblade at a 45° angle and raise it to a height of ½ in. above the saw table as shown in the photo above right. Pass the finial board through the saw–

Finial measurements

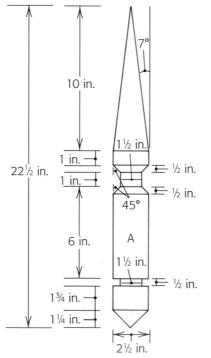

Use a tapering jig to make four 7° cuts at the top of the finial.

Tilt the sawblade 45° to create the chamfer around the middle of the finial.

The final set of sawcuts creates the point at the base.

blade on four sides in one direction, then flip the board over and make the other side of the chamfer. Return the blade to its normal vertical position and set it to a height of ½ in. Now cut out the area between the chamfered cuts by passing the board through the sawblade several times on each side. When you are finished trimming out the chamfered groove, use the same sawblade setting to trim out the ½–in. groove near the base of the finial.

The final set of saw cuts creates the point at the base. Until now, you've been working with a 24-in. length of board, which made it easier to handle in the tapering jig. The last set of miter cuts trims the length of the finial to its final dimension of 22½ in. To do this, raise the sawblade to about 3 in. and set the miter gauge to 45°. Pencil mark four lines around the base of the finial 21¼ in. below the tip of the spire. This is where you will start the four 45° bevel cuts at the bottom of the finial. Hold the finial against the miter gauge as shown

Nearly 2 ft. tall, the decorative finial stands out against the blue sky.

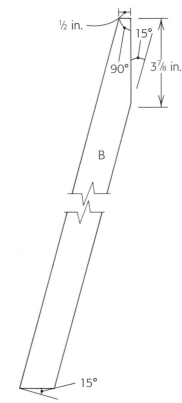

Leg measurements

½ in.

15°

90°

3⅞ in.

B

15°

in the bottom right photo on p. 41, then pass the finial through the sawblade on all four sides. Once the cutting is complete, sand all surfaces of the finial until smooth and apply the finish of your choice.

2 Cut the four trellis legs (B) using the dimensions and angles shown in the illustration above. From a standard 8–ft. length of cedar 2x2, first make the 15° taper cut at the top of the leg with a tapering jig. Then make the remaining two angle cuts, which will trim the leg to its proper length. Cut the other three legs following the same procedure, using the first leg as a template. The exact length of the legs isn't as important as having them all match.

3 Once the finial and legs are cut, apply paint or stain before you assemble the pieces. This will make it easier to reach the lower parts of the finial, which will be partially covered by the four legs. We first applied a clear waterproofing coat, then finished it with a solid–color stain.

4 Attach the four legs to the finial in the 6–in. flat area directly below the spire (see the illustration on the facing page). With the help of an assistant, lay the finial down on a smooth, flat surface and position the first leg as shown. Once in place, predrill and countersink the holes for the two attachment screws (C, D). The 1½–in. screw installs in the top hole and the 2½–in. screw in the bottom.

You can attach three of the four legs with the trellis lying on its side, but the fourth leg should be installed with the trellis standing upright.

5 If you plan to disassemble the trellis at the end of the season, leave the screws unpainted to make it easier to back them out. If you will leave the trellis out in the garden year–round, as we do, you may want to fill the screw holes and touch them up with some paint or stain.

6 Lastly, install the trellis in the gar–den. After choosing the location for the trellis, pound two small stakes in the ground near opposing legs and lash the trellis to the stakes. This will stabilize it against any high winds until the vines have had a chance to wrap themselves around the legs.

Leg and finial attachment

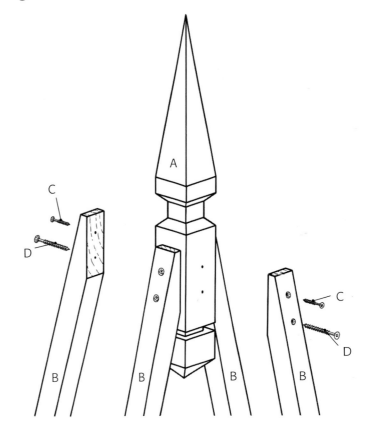

Placed in the center of a vegetable bed, the trellis becomes a focal point.

PLANTER BOX AND OBELISK

Strategically placed on a terrace, in a garden, or at the axis of two converging paths, this classic Planter Box and Obelisk combination is an elegant garden accent year-round. Whether it's supporting rambling roses or morning glory vines during the summer or standing bare during the winter, this project always contributes architectural structure to the landscape.

If you prefer, the components of this two-in-one project can be used separately. The classical styling of the Planter Box makes it the perfect container for a small tree or a lush display of summer annuals. The Obelisk is about 6½ ft. tall and perfectly proportioned to stand on its own as a centerpiece in a flower or vegetable garden. Used separately or in combination, this project will convey a feeling of formality and is reminiscent of bygone days.

Add a touch of formality to your landscape with this traditionally styled Planter Box and Obelisk.

PLANTER BOX AND OBELISK MATERIALS LIST

Key	Qty.	Description	Finished Dimensions	Material
Planter Box				
A	4	Corner posts	3½ in. x 3½ in. x 28 in.	Cedar
B	4	Top rails	1½ in. x 3½ in. x 24 in.	Cedar
C	4	Bottom rails	1½ in. x 3½ in. x 24 in.	Cedar
D	8	Side rails	1½ in. x 1½ in. x 15 in.	Cedar
E	16	Center panels	11/16 in. x 5¼ in. x 15¾ in.	Cedar (T&G siding)
F	4	Floor supports	¾ in. x 1½ in. x 22 in.	Cedar
G	6	Floorboards	1½ in. x 3½ in. x 23⅞ in.	Cedar
H	1	Floorboard	1½ in. x 1½ in. x 23⅞ in.	Cedar
I	4	Corner braces	1½ in. x 3½ in. x 8½ in. (before mitering)	Cedar
J	4	Fence-post finials	2¾ in. x 4¼ in.	Cedar
K	54	Outdoor screws	#8 x 2½ in.	Stainless steel or galvanized
L	12	Outdoor screws	#8 x 2 in.	Stainless steel or galvanized
Obelisk				
A	1	Table leg	2¼ in. x 2¼ in. x 15¼ in.	Premade (French style)
B	1	Wooden drawer knob	2 in. round	Premade (white birch)
C	4	Legs	1½ in. x 1½ in. x 75¾ in.	Cedar
D	4	Upper lath supports	¾ in. x 1½ in. x 9¼ in. (before mitering)	Cedar
E	4	Lower lath supports	¾ in. x 1½ in. x 15⅞ in. (before mitering)	Cedar
F	4	Middle lath pieces	¼ in. x 1½ in. x 48 in.	Poplar
G	8	Side lath pieces	¼ in. x 1½ in. x 36 in.	Poplar
H	1	Dowel screw	3/16 in. x 2 in.	Galvanized
I	4	Hanger bolts	¼–20 x 3 in.	Galvanized
J	4	Washers	¼ in.	Galvanized
K	4	Nuts	¼-in. hex	Galvanized
L	16	Outdoor screws	#8 x 1½ in.	Galvanized or stainless steel
M	24	Outdoor screws	#6 x ¾ in.	Galvanized or stainless steel

PLANTER BOX ASSEMBLY

The Planter Box is constructed using a series of mortise–and–tenon joints for strength. All four sides are identical, making it easier to precut your pieces before you begin. Two opposing sides of the box are built first, then joined together by the remaining two sides. Once the four sides are assembled, corner braces and a floor are added. With the addition of a set of fence-post finials, this Planter Box can be enjoyed as is or combined with the Obelisk for a striking garden centerpiece.

1 At one end of each of the four corner posts (A), cut a ½–in. chamfer on all sides. This should leave the top of each post with a measurement of 2½ in. by 2½ in., which is the typical diameter of the base of most round fence-post finials.

2 Once the top is chamfered, create four 1–in.–deep mortises on each post that will accept the matching tenons of the top and bottom 2x4 side rails (B, C), as shown in the illustration at top right.

3 Cut to size the top, bottom, and side rails (B, C, D) for all four sides of the planter box. On the top and bottom rails, make 1–in.–long tenon cuts at each end. (For more information on mortise-and-tenon joints, see the sidebar on p. 77.) After making the tenons, cut a ½–in.–deep by ¾–in.–wide groove down one side of each top and bottom rail (see the illustration at bottom right). This groove will hold the four sections of cedar tongue-and-groove siding that make up the middle panel of each completed side. Then make the same dimension groove down the center of each side rail. Attach the side rails to the

Side wall assembly

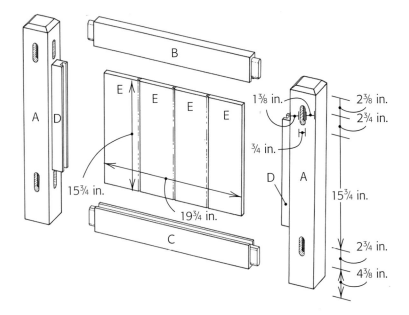

Top and bottom rail construction

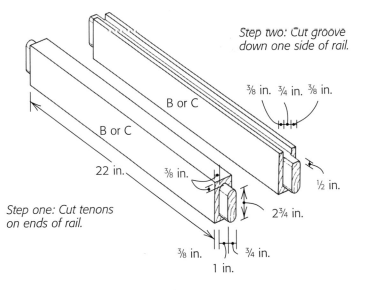

Step two: Cut groove down one side of rail.

Step one: Cut tenons on ends of rail.

Box assembly

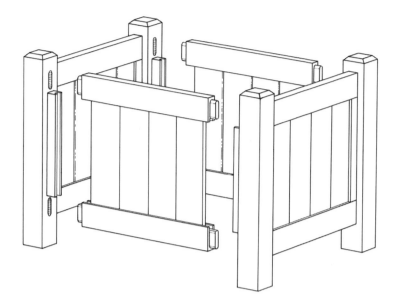

Laying in floor boards

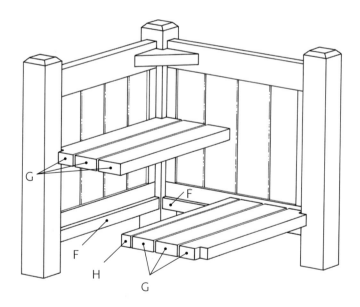

posts with two outdoor screws (K). Predrill and countersink the holes, then drive the screws from within the groove into the corner posts (see the top illustration on p. 47).

4 Put the four pieces of the tongue-and-groove siding (E) together so you have one interlocking panel. After measuring the total length of the panel, trim off an equal amount from the two outside pieces so the final panel dimension is 15¾ in. by 19¾ in. (about ¼ in. cut from both sides).

5 Apply an outdoor wood glue to all mortise-and-tenon surfaces before assembling the pieces for the first two sides of the planter box. Use pipe clamps to hold each side securely together until the glue has dried overnight.

6 Repeat these same steps to install the final two sides (see the illustration at top left). Since the first two sides and the last two sides will have to be assembled at the same time, have an assistant help you guide all of the pieces into position until the last two sides can be clamped. Again, let the glue dry overnight before continuing.

7 To secure the mortise-and-tenon joints further, install 16 screws (K) along the inside edges of the corner posts to lock the tenons in place. Use one screw for each tenon.

8 Next, install the four floorboard supports (F) and the seven floorboards (G, H) as shown in the illustration at bottom left. Each floorboard support is attached to the lower edge of a bottom rail (C) with three screws (L). Note that the two outside floorboards need to have a 1-in. notch cut out on each end to clear the four corner posts. Once in place, there should be a ¼-in. gap between each of the seven floorboards. When you have the spacing about even, secure the floorboards with one screw (K) at either end of each board.

9 Cut out the four corner braces (I) as shown in the illustration at top right. The planter box will need the braces whether or not you decide to install the obelisk top. If you are going to install the obelisk, drill a ⅜-in. hole about 1 in. from the notch, as shown in the top left illustration on p. 50. On the bottom side of each corner brace, drill a ⅞-in. hole about ¾ in. deep centered on the ⅜-in. hole you just drilled. These holes will accept the hanger bolts, washers, and nuts for the obelisk legs. To install the corner braces, set them in position and predrill two holes for screws (K) about 1 in. from each end. Drive in two screws per brace (see the illustration at bottom right).

10 Attach the four fence-post finials (J) on the top of each corner post. These premade finials will give the planter-box corners a turned look without the need for a lathe. Finials are normally sold with a dowel screw already installed, making it easy to attach them to the corner posts. To do this, find the center point on the top of each post and drill a ³⁄₁₆-in. hole deep enough to accept the dowel screw. Then twist the finials on until they are snug.

Corner brace grid

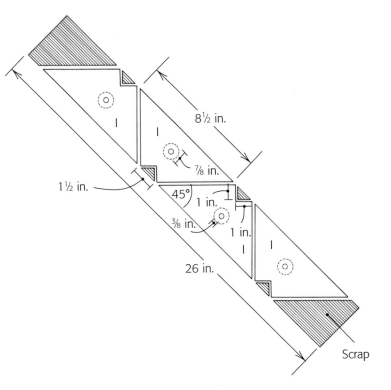

Installation of corner braces and finial balls

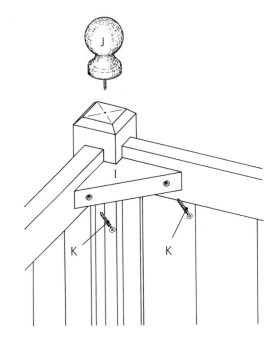

Drill hole placement in corner brace and obelisk leg

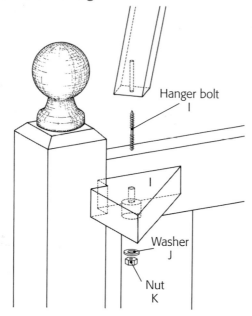

Hanger bolt
I

I

Washer
J

Nut
K

Final preparation of obelisk

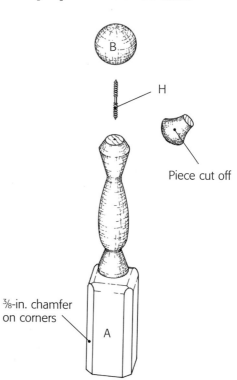

B

H

Piece cut off

⅜-in. chamfer
on corners

A

Obelisk leg measurements

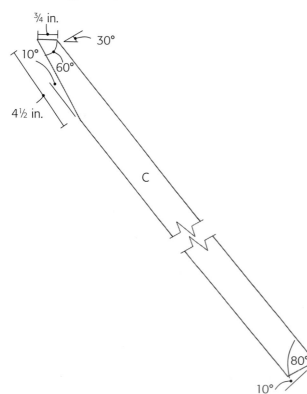

¾ in.

30°

10°

60°

4½ in.

C

80°

10°

Obelisk leg attachment to finial base

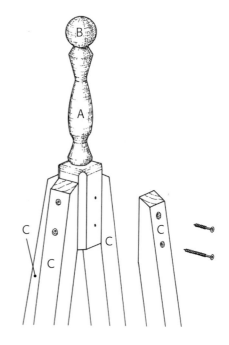

B

A

C

C

C

C

11 With the assembly finished, sand any rough spots and finish with your choice of a paint or stain. Let the planter box stand for several days to allow the finish to cure before filling it with a good potting soil mix.

OBELISK ASSEMBLY

Many wooden obelisks are built around an expensive finial, normally purchased through a mail-order catalog. We decided to look for an alternative that would be equally attractive, less expensive, and readily available. Our solution was to use a country French-style table leg that we found at our local home center. To make it less recognizable as a table leg, we cut off the tapered foot section and replaced it with a round, wooden drawer knob. By combining the resulting finial with four legs and some decorative lath, we created a beautiful obelisk that can be used alone or combined with the planter box for a great addition to any garden.

1 Start by preparing the finial (A). Most home centers carry a good assortment of premade table legs. While we chose a country French-style leg, you may find another style that better suits your tastes. We first cut off the tapered foot at one end of the leg, then drilled a $\frac{1}{8}$-in. hole to accept a dowel screw (H), as shown in the illustration at top right on the facing page. After installing one-half of the dowel screw into the table leg, we attached the 2-in. round, wooden drawer knob (B) onto the remaining part of the screw (these round knobs come predrilled on one side). Then we made a $\frac{3}{8}$-in. chamfer along the four corners of the leg's base. Each flat side of the base was now 1½ in.

This finial may look expensive but it's actually constructed from an inexpensive table leg and a drawer knob.

wide, the same width as the four obelisk legs.

2 Cut the four obelisk legs (C) to size, as shown in the illustration at bottom left on the facing page. If you are going to mount the obelisk to the planter box, drill a $\frac{3}{16}$-in. hole about 1½ in. deep in the bottom of each leg. A doweling jig works well to keep the drill bit perpendicular to the bottom surface while drilling (see the sidebar on doweling on p. 63). With a pair of pliers, twist the screw end of the hanger bolt (I) into the leg, leaving the bolt end protruding. Don't install the hanger bolts if you won't be mounting the obelisk onto the planter box.

3 Attach the legs to the finial base as shown in the illustration at bottom right on the facing page (for details, see the Pole Bean Trellis assembly instructions

The obelisk legs easily bolt to the corners of the planter box.

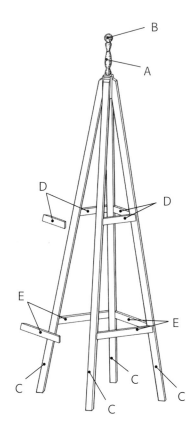

on pp. 40–43). Proceed to step 5 if you are not mounting the obelisk to the planter box.

4 Once the legs are secured to the finial, set the obelisk onto the corner braces of the planter box (see the top left illustration on p. 50). Guide the four hanger bolts into the ⅜–in. holes, and secure them from the underside of the braces with washers and hex nuts (J, K).

5 Miter and attach the upper and lower lath supports (D, E) to the obelisk frame. Set your table saw blade to a 45° angle and your miter gauge to 85°, then trim the supports to length as shown in the illustration above. Because there is room for variation depending on the exact placement of the legs and the

trueness of the leg boards, you may want to cut a test piece for both the upper and lower lath support pieces to ensure a proper fit.

6 Attach the lath support pieces to the obelisk legs using outdoor screws (L). Each lath support is held in place by one screw at each end. To prevent split–ting the wood, predrill and countersink the screw holes.

7 Once all eight lath support pieces are in place, cut the middle and side lath pieces (F, G) to size, as shown in the illustration at left on the facing page. Mount the lath pieces to the lath sup–

Obelisk lath measurements

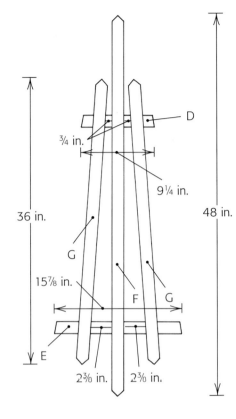

3/4 in.

9 1/4 in.

36 in.

48 in.

D

G

15 7/8 in.

F   G

E

2 3/8 in.   2 3/8 in.

The decorative lath panels give extra vertical support to vigorous vines.

Obelisk separated from Planter Box

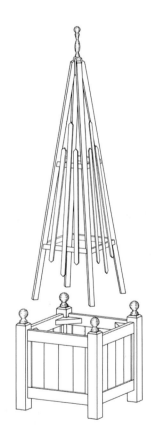

ports with two outdoor screws (M). When all of the lath pieces are in place, you can carefully back the screws out of the lath supports and remove all four sections for painting or staining. Make sure you keep track of the position of each section, as they will vary slightly. When the finish has dried, replace all four sections.

Its versatility makes this project appealing. Even if you decide to mount the Obelisk on top of the Planter Box, you can easily separate the two pieces in the future if your garden design changes. The only remaining task is to determine the perfect garden location for your new Planter Box and Obelisk.

3

Tables, Benches, and Plant Stands

Gardeners need work areas specifically designed for their activities. Flat surfaces are most useful, but they must withstand the two main ingredients of gardening: soil and water. The following projects offer a variety of surfaces for propagating, displaying, and enjoying plants. Each is a classic design built with modern, water–resistant hardware and finishes. This chapter includes plans for a Greenhouse Table and Potting Bench for plant propagation, a Rolling Bench and Potted Plant Stand for displays, and finally a Vegetable Washstand for preparing vegetables and cut flowers.

GREENHOUSE TABLE

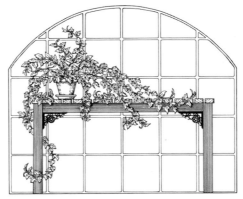

If you've built an elegant greenhouse such as the one on pp. 118–139, the tables inside should complement the structure's craftsmanship. This easy-to-build Greenhouse Table is sturdy yet tasteful and will also be at home in a potting shed or breezeway. The decorative iron brackets add to its strength while contributing a touch of charm. The table is constructed from water-resistant cedar and preserved with an exterior oil-based stain, which allows you to place potted plants and flats directly on its surface. Excess water and soil easily drain and fall through the gaps between the slatted tabletop boards. The simple design of the bench makes it easy to customize its length and height to fit into any size greenhouse and be a comfortable work height for any gardener. With minimal maintenance, this wooden bench will beautifully stage your plants and give years of service.

Made from rot-resistant cedar and finished with an oil-based stain, this Greenhouse Table will last for years and beautifully display your plants.

TABLES, BENCHES, AND PLANT STANDS **57**

GREENHOUSE TABLE MATERIALS LIST

Key	Qty.	Description	Finished Dimensions	Material
A	2	Top rails	1½ in. x 3½ in. x 87 in.	Cedar
B	4	Legs	1½ in. x 3½ in. x 35 in.	Cedar
C	5	Spanner boards	1½ in. x 3½ in. x 19¼ in.	Cedar
D	24	Table boards	1 in. x 3½ in. x 23¾ in.	Cedar
E*	8	Dowel pins	⅜ in. x 2½ in.	Hardwood
F*	20	Dowel plugs	⅜ in. x ¼ in.	Hardwood
G*	118	Wood screws	8 in. x 2½ in.	Stainless steel or silicon bronze
H*	4	Brackets	6¾ in. x 9 in.	Cast iron (including screws)

*See project resources on p. 179.

Greenhouse Table leg assembly

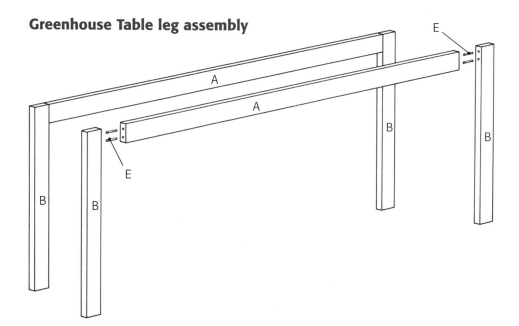

A well-loved and often-used green-house demands a worktable that can hold its own against constant watering and spilled potting soil, so we designed this Greenhouse Table with that in mind. The length of the table is easily adjusted. Simply subtract 4 in. from the top rails for each table board you remove. Then recenter the middle span-ner board between the two top rails.

1 Begin by making the two frames shown in the illustration on the facing page. The top rails (A) are attached to the leg boards (B) with two hardwood dowels (E) at each joint. Use a doweling jig to accurately place the dowel holes, then apply waterproof wood glue to both the holes and the dowels. Tap the dowels into the top rail about halfway, and attach the leg to the rail.

Closeup view of the Greenhouse Table dowel joint

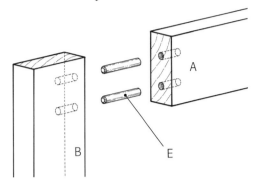

2 After completing each frame, attach a piece of scrap 1x2 near each leg/rail joint to keep the legs square to the rail while finishing the project. Attach the 1x2s with wood screws on the inside

Greenhouse Table frame assembly

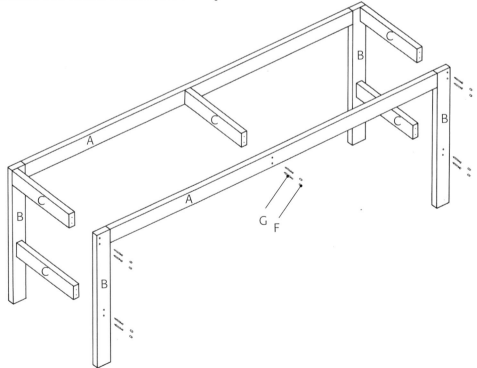

Closeup view of the Greenhouse Table screw attachment

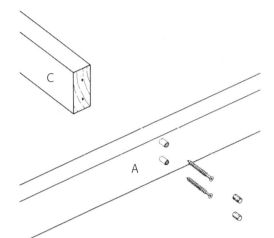

The tabletop boards are gapped to allow water to easily drain.

edges so the screw holes won't show once the braces are removed.

3 When both frames have had at least 24 hours to dry, begin installing the five spanner boards (C), as shown in the bottom illustration on p. 59. The two outside frames are connected to the spanner boards using two wood screws (G) at each joint. We found it helpful to place the two table frames on another table that is slightly higher (this will suspend the legs just off the ground, making it easier to position both frames while attaching the five spanner boards).

Installation of the Greenhouse Table brackets and tabletop boards

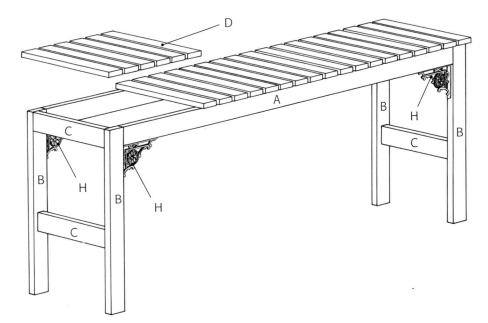

4 To secure each spanner–board joint, drill two ⅜-in. holes about ¾ in. deep (see the illustration on the facing page). Install one screw into each hole until it is firmly seated.

5 Once the table frame is assembled and standing on its own, install the 24 table boards (D) that make up the work surface. The table boards overhang the completed frame by ¾ in. on all sides. There is also a ½-in. space between each board. Start by securing the two end table boards to the table frame with three screws, one at each end and one in the middle, centered above

the outside spanner board. Next, rip a piece of scrap 1x2 (about the same length as the table boards) to a width of ½ in. Use this as a spacer to keep a consistent gap between the table boards. Lay out all of the table boards and adjust the spacing if necessary. Once you have them all lined up and even, secure each one with four wood screws (G)—two at either end and centered over the two top rails.

6 Fill the exposed ⅜-in. screw holes in the table frame with ⅜-in. dowel plugs (F), adding a little waterproof wood glue to the plugs before tapping them into

Decorative brackets support the corners and add detail to this simple table design.

place. Once the glue is dry, apply either a waterproofing sealer or exterior oil–based wood stain.

7 Finish the table by adding four brackets (H) to the corners of the table frame (see the illustration on p. 61). While these brackets give the frame some additional strength, we installed them primarily for their decorative value. Spray the brackets with a coat or two of paint before installation to help prevent rust. Once completed, use the table to hold a collection of beautiful potted plants or eight standard seedling flats.

Dowel Joints

One of our favorite ways to create a simple yet strong wood joint is to use hardwood dowels. Many of the projects in this book take advantage of this type of joint, including the Greenhouse, Greenhouse Table, and Rolling Bench.

Making this joint is fairly simple with the help of a doweling jig. These jigs come in a few different styles, but all do basically the same thing—help you drill a straight hole at precisely the right spot. Specific instructions for using each particular jig are included with the tool. The following steps will help you make an accurate doweled joint every time.

1. Position the two pieces you want to join as they will be in the finished project. Make two pencil marks on the wood indicating the location of the dowel pins, as shown in the photo at right.

2. Use these marks to position the doweling jig at the correct spot on both boards. After tightening the jig, drill a hole using a bit of the same size as the dowel pins. Drill to a depth that is slightly more than one-half the length of the dowel pin.

3. Spread wood glue evenly in each hole. Coat one-half of each dowel pin with glue and insert the pins into the holes in one of the boards. Use a rubber mal-

let if they need coaxing (a snug fit is preferable). Next, coat the remaining half of each dowel pin and insert the pins into the other board. If necessary, use a mallet to tap the two pieces together.

4. Once your doweled frame is complete, lightly clamp it and set it aside to dry for at least 24 hours.

Create a simple yet strong wood joint using hardwood dowels and a doweling jig.

POTTING BENCH

There comes a point when every gardener tires of using the kitchen counter or the tool bench in the garage as a potting bench. If that point has arrived for you, consider making this traditional Potting Bench.

Perhaps its best component is the durable galvanized tray. The tray's tall sides keep potting soil from spilling off the work surface. Shelves above and below the work surface can hold a variety of tools and supplies such as pots, flats, fertilizer, and soil. We added three antique reproduction hooks for hanging often-used items such as scissors, twine, or a trowel. So if the kitchen counter is not your ideal garden work space, consider building this deluxe Potting Bench and make your planting and potting jobs enjoyable.

The design of this Potting Bench is straightforward with ample room on the work surface, but we decided to take the

If you construct this classic Potting Bench, you'll never have to pot a plant on your kitchen counter again.

POTTING BENCH MATERIALS LIST

Key	Qty.	Description	Finished Dimensions	Material
A	2	Rear legs	1½ in. x 3½ in. x 54 in.	Cedar
B	2	Front legs	1½ in. x 3½ in. x 35¼ in.	Cedar
C	2	Upper-leg spanner boards	1½ in. x 3½ in. x 21¾ in.	Cedar
D	2	Lower-leg spanner boards	1½ in. x 3½ in. x 24¾ in.	Cedar
E	1	Work surface	¾ in. x 23¼ in. x 46½ in.	ADX plywood
F	1	Back board	¾ in. x 5¼ in. x 46½ in.	Cedar
G	1	Front trim board	¾ in. x 1½ in. x 46½ in.	Cedar
H	2	Side boards	¾ in. x 7½ in. x 25½ in.	Cedar
I	6	Lower shelf boards	1½ in. x 3½ in. x 46½ in.	Cedar
J	1	Hook board	¾ in. x 5½ in. x 46½ in.	Cedar
K	1	Top shelf board	¾ in. x 7½ in. x 48 in.	Cedar
L	2	Shelf supports	¾ in. x 7 in. x 7 in.	Cedar
M	1	Tray	5 in. x 23¼ in. x 46⅜ in.	Galvanized sheet metal
N*	40	Wood screws	#8 x 2½ in.	Stainless steel
O*	36	Wood screws	#8 x 2 in.	Stainless steel
P*	16	Pan-head screws	#6 x ¾ in.	Stainless steel
Q*	3	Hooks	3 in.	Cast iron

*See project resources on p. 179.

bench one step further by adding an attractive yet practical galvanized metal tray. Because the tray is added last, you can choose to include it or not.

We had the tray made to order at a local sheet–metal fabrication shop. The simple bends and corner welds proved no problem for professionals used to creating more complicated heating and cooling ducts. If you have the tray made, make sure the fabricator drills the screw holes for mounting the tray to the work surface. It then takes just a few minutes to set the tray in place and install the screws.

If you decide to have the tray made, copy the top illustration on the facing page and the bottom illustration on p. 69 to leave with the fabricator so he can properly size the tray. It should be ¹⁄₁₆ in. to ⅛ in. smaller than the width of the work surface to easily slide into place with a snug fit. Alternately, you could have the tray made first so you

The galvanized tray makes a durable and long-lasting work surface.

Potting Bench galvanized tray template

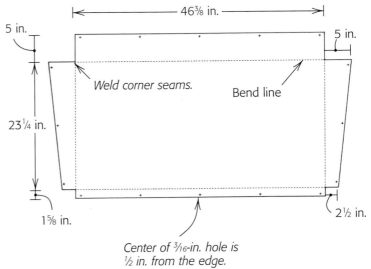

46³⁄₈ in.

5 in.

5 in.

Weld corner seams.

Bend line

23¹⁄₄ in.

1⁵⁄₈ in.

2¹⁄₂ in.

Center of ³⁄₁₆-in. hole is ¹⁄₂ in. from the edge.

Potting Bench leg assembly

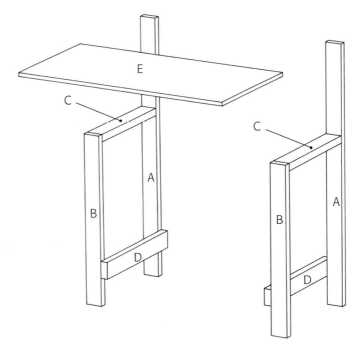

can make any small adjustments to the size of the work surface if the tray is a little off.

1 Begin assembly by making the two end frames comprised of boards (A, B, C, D), as shown in the illustration at right. Both the upper–leg spanner boards and the lower–leg spanner boards attach to the legs using two wood screws (N) at each joint. As always, predrill and countersink the screw holes to prevent splitting the wood.

2 Stand both completed end frames on level ground, then lay the work surface plywood (E) on top of the upper–leg spanner boards and front legs. The back of the work surface butts up against the rear legs, while the sides are flush with

Potting Bench assembly of shelves, brackets, and side boards

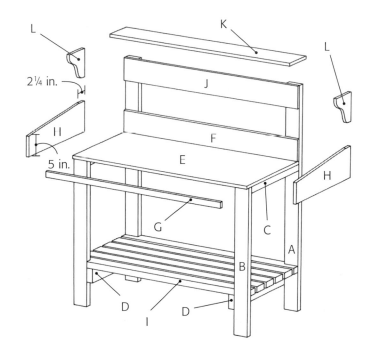

the outside edges of the legs and upper-leg spanner boards. Attach the work surface with three wood screws (O) on each side.

3 Next, attach the back board (F), front trim board (G), and side boards (H), as shown in the illustration at left. The back board attaches to the rear legs with two screws (O) at either end. The front trim board attaches to the front legs with two screws (O) at either end as well. Also, drive three evenly spaced screws (O) through the front edge of the work surface and into the top of the front trim board. Finally, attach the two side boards (H) to the front and rear legs with two screws (O) at either end. Drive one additional screw (O) into the upper-leg spanner board from the middle of each side board. Notice that there is a tapered cut on the top of each side board. You can make this cut with a circular saw and a straightedge or by using a tapering jig on a table saw.

4 Once the work surface is framed in, add the lower shelf boards (I). They bridge the lower-leg spanner boards and provide a convenient place to store supplies. Each lower shelf board is secured with two wood screws (N) at each end. The two outside shelf boards are notched to fit around the front and rear legs (see the illustration at left) and each board is separated by a gap of ¾ in. Once the shelf boards are installed, the bench becomes very stable.

5 The final set of boards to be installed makes up the shelf above the work surface. Start by attaching the hook board (J) to the top of the rear legs with two screws (O) at either end. The top shelf board (K) goes on next using

The sturdy bottom shelf easily holds the weight of pots, supplies, and potting soil.

four screws (O). Two are installed into the tops of the rear legs and two are installed into the top edge of the hook board. The final two boards are the shelf support boards (L). Use the grid pattern at top right to make the support boards, then install each one with two screws (O), driving them into the edge of the rear legs. Use one more screw (O) per board to lock the end of the shelf board to the support board. Drive these screws through the top shelf board (near the front), then into the shelf support board.

6 With the bench complete except for adding the galvanized tray, apply your choice of finish. We brushed on a semi-transparent oil-based stain, the same one we used for our greenhouse and greenhouse tables.

7 Install the tray (M) and secure it with the 14 pan-head screws (P), as shown in the illustration at bottom right. If you decide not to include the tray, simply add a strip of screen molding (a common 1/8-in. by 3/4-in. molding) to the raw edge on the front of the work surface plywood (E). Otherwise, the galvanized tray will cover this unfinished edge.

8 Install the hooks (Q) on the hook board. A wide variety of hooks can be used, but we chose three cast-iron hooks that lend an old-fashioned feel to the bench. As with other types of cast-iron fixtures though, always add two or three more coats of paint to help protect them from rust corrosion. This is especially important in a greenhouse or outdoors. If you use brass or stainless steel hooks, you won't have a problem with rust.

Potting Bench shelf support grid

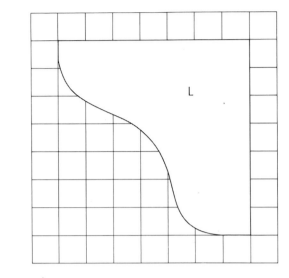

1 square = 1 in.

Inserting the tray on the Potting Bench

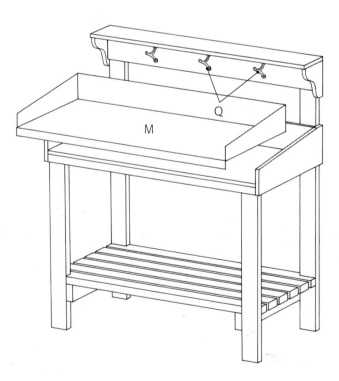

Reminiscent of an old-fashioned flower vendor's cart, this Rolling Bench has multiple uses. It displays flowers and potted plants during the spring and summer and colorful gourds and pumpkins in the fall. Used as a rustic buffet table, it's indispensable for barbecues and outdoor entertaining. It can even double as a movable potting bench; flats of young seedlings can be rolled into the shade during the hottest hours of the day.

Old metal wheels give this Rolling Bench its classic charm. Similar wheels can often be found at country auctions or in rural antique shops, however, new 26-in. cart wheels are just as functional and readily available. If you construct this Rolling Bench, you may discover it is one of the most often-used accessories in your garden.

Although we designed the Rolling Bench to use two 26-in. garden cart

This versatile Rolling Bench may quickly become one of the most-often-used accessories in your garden.

ROLLING BENCH MATERIALS LIST

Key	Qty.	Description	Finished Dimensions	Material
A	14	Table boards	1 in. x 3½ in. x 29½ in.	Cedar
B	2	Side rails	1½ in. x 3½ in. x 54 in.	Cedar
C	2	End rails	1½ in. x 3½ in. x 25 in.	Cedar
D	2	Rear legs	1½ in. x 3½ in. x 35 in.	Cedar
E	2	Handle supports	1½ in. x 3½ in. x 11 in.	Cedar
F	1	Leg spanner board	1½ in. x 5½ in. x 22 in.	Cedar
G	2	Leg braces	1½ in. x 3½ in. x 53¾ in.	Cedar
H	2	Wheel support boards	1½ in. x 3½ in. x 48 in.	Cedar
I	2	Handles	1½ in. x 1½ in. x 48½ in.	Commercially made
J*	4	Dowel pins	⅜ in. x 2½ in.	Hardwood
K*	58	Wood screws	#8 x 2½ in.	Stainless steel or silicon bronze
L*	2	Wheels	26 in. to 30 in.	Antique or modern
M	4	Carriage bolts	⅜-20 x 5½ in.	Galvanized
N	8	Carriage bolts	⅜-20 x 4 in.	Galvanized
O	12	Washers	⅜ in. (I.D.)	Galvanized
P	12	Hex nuts	⅜-20	Galvanized
Q	1	Axle	Length depends on wheels	Galvanized
R	2	Wheel retainers	Depends on axle	Galvanized
S	2	Wheel bushings	Depends on axle	Galvanized
T	4	Mending Plates	1 in. x 9 in.	Galvanized
U	8	Hex bolts	¼-20 x 4½ in.	Galvanized
V	8	Lock washers	¼ in. (I.D.)	Galvanized
W	8	Hex nuts	¼-20	Galvanized

*See project resources on p. 179.

Rolling Bench bench top assembly

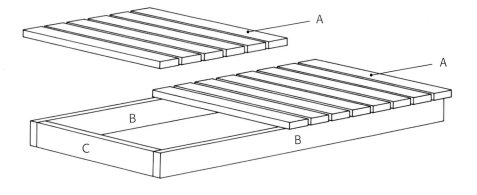

wheels, you can add to the classic feel of the bench by searching for a pair of antique metal wheels. We paid $25 dol-lars for a pair of wheels that the dealer removed from an old rusted cement mixer (we suspect there were two very happy parties in this transaction). After having them sandblasted, we spray painted them to match the weathered barnboard stain we chose for the bench.

The particular axle you use for the bench will depend on the type of wheels you decide on. We found that a 1-in. galvanized pipe fit our wheels per-fectly. Threaded pipe caps hold the wheels in place. If you choose a more modern garden cart wheel (see resources on p. 178), use an appropriate size threaded rod inserted into an aluminum tube. Retain this type of wheel with cap nuts and washers.

1 Cut all of the individual boards to size except for the wheelbarrow handles (I), which can be purchased from most hardware stores or home centers. Wait until you are ready to install the handles before trimming them to length.

Rolling Bench leg assembly

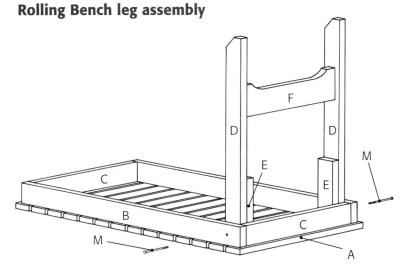

2 Construct the bench tabletop by attaching side rails (B) to end rails (C), using two wood screws (K) at each joint. Then attach the table boards (A) to the frame, as shown in the top illustration. Each table board is secured with two wood screws (K) on each end. The two end table boards are secured with one screw at each end and two in the middle, which are centered over the end rails.

3 Invert the completed tabletop on a flat, smooth surface, as shown in the bottom illustration on p. 73. The rest of the rolling bench frame will attach to the underside of the tabletop.

4 Cut a chamfer at the end of both rear legs, then make the rear leg assembly. We attached the leg spanner board (F) to the two rear legs (D) using two mortise-and-tenon joints (see the sidebar on p. 77). However, you can attach the leg spanner board using two wood screws on each side, similar to what we did with the Greenhouse Table (see pp. 56–62). Before attaching the spanner board, use a sabersaw to cut away a simple scallop.

5 With the two legs attached to the leg spanner board, set this H-shaped assembly in place within the two side rails, as shown in the bottom illustration on p. 73. Then set the two handle support boards (E) in place. Use a large C-clamp or bar clamp to hold the side rail, rear leg, and handle support board

together as you drill a ⅜-in. hole on each side for two carriage bolts (M). Secure each side with one carriage bolt, washer (O), and hex nut (P). For extra strength, install one wood screw (K) through each handle support board and into the rear legs at the opposite end from where you installed the carriage bolt.

6 Make the angle cuts on both leg braces (G), as shown in the illustration at left. The 60° cut is made at the leg end of both leg braces, while the 30° cut is made at the opposite end. Two dowels (J) connect each leg brace to the rear legs (see the sidebar on p. 63). The other end of the leg brace sits against the underside of the table boards and is secured to the side rail with one carriage bolt (N), washer (O), and hex nut (P).

7 The next set of boards to install are the wheel support boards (H). One end of these two boards remains squared off, while the other end has two angle cuts, as shown in the illustration at left. Once you have cut the angles on one side of these boards and set them in place, the wheel support boards should be at a 24½° angle in relation to the side rail board. Before drilling the two carriage bolt holes in each of these two boards, clamp them in place using two C-clamps or bar clamps. The shorter carriage bolt (N) joins the leg brace and wheel support boards, while the longer bolt (M) joins one end of the wheel support board to the rear leg assembly.

8 Once these boards are bolted in place, determine where to drill the axle holes for the size of wheel (L) you are going to install by using the radius measurement of the wheel (see the illustra-

Rolling Bench axle support leg assembly

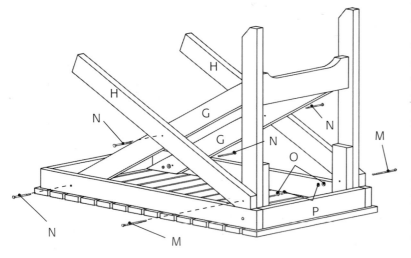

tion at right). For instance, a 26-in. wheel would place the axle hole 13 in. from the front edge of the table and 13 in. from the bottom of the rear leg (the chamfered end of the leg). To make sure the hole is centered in the wheel support board, adjust the distance from the front of the table. The size of axle hole can only be determined after you have selected the wheels and determined the size and type of axle (Q) you will use.

9 To prevent the wheel support board from splitting while using the rolling bench, add two 9-in. mending plates (T) at the wheel end of each board (see the top illustration on p. 76). These galvanized plates are available at most hardware stores and serve to hold together the wood around the axle. Place one plate on either side of each wheel support board, then adjust the plates so they are centered over the axle hole. Next, pencil mark the position of four holes in each of the mending plates (two on either side of the axle hole). Remove the plate and, with a drill guide, drill a ¼-in. hole through the wheel support board at each pencil mark. Position the mending plates, and insert four ¼-in. hex bolts (U) through the holes. Fasten the other ends with lock washers (V) and hex nuts (W).

10 Before you install the wheels and turn the rolling bench right side up, install the two handles (I). To do this, rest each handle on the handle support board with the tapered end 18 in. from the rear leg. Hold the other end of the handle against the inside edge of the leg brace, making sure it is parallel with the side rail below it. On the handle, pencil mark the position of the angle cut needed to trim the handle to the length shown in the bottom illustration on

Rolling Bench wheel alignment

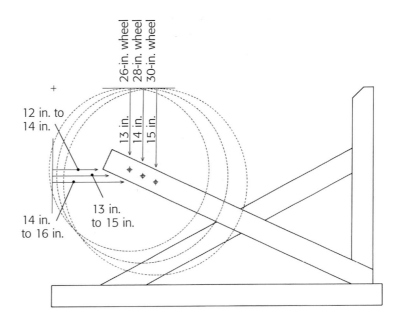

26-in. wheel
28-in. wheel
30-in. wheel

12 in. to 14 in.

13 in.
14 in.
15 in.

14 in. to 16 in.

13 in. to 15 in.

p. 76. Trim the other handle in the same way. Next, clamp the ends of the handles to the leg braces, resting the other end of the handle on the handle support boards. Drill ⅜-in. holes through the handles, leg braces, and rear

For easy construction, the Rolling Bench uses commercially made wheelbarrow handles.

Closeup of mending plate supports

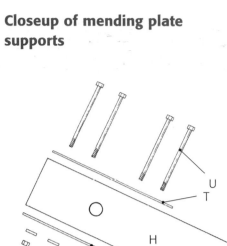

legs, as shown in the illustration below, then secure the handles with four car-riage bolts (N).

11 Install the wheels and axle you have chosen. If you are using a pipe axle, retain the wheel with a threaded

pipe cap (R) and separate the wheel from the wheel support board with a galvanized bushing (S). If you are using a threaded rod and tube axle, use a threaded cap nut (R) to retain the wheel and a large galvanized washer (S) to separate the wheel from the wheel sup-port board. With the wheels and handles in place, have someone help you turn the Rolling Bench right side up. If the placement of the wheels was measured correctly, the work surface should be fairly level.

12 Finally, apply a good coat of waterproofing sealer or oil–based stain. Once the finish is dry, you can use the Rolling Bench as a portable worktable, plant stand, or for a variety of other uses in and around the garden.

Rolling Bench wheel attachment

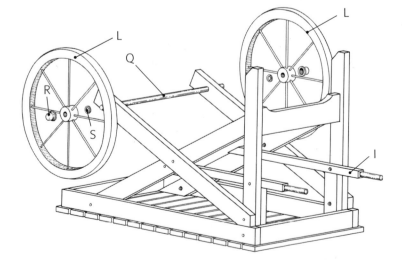

Use antique metal wheels for a bench with an old-fashioned feel. Alternately, you can purchase lightweight garden-cart wheels through catalogs or at some home centers.

Mortise-and-tenon joints are widely used in woodworking because they are strong and relatively easy to make. The illustration at right outlines the basic steps to make both parts.

Tenon

1. Pencil mark the exact location of the tenon at the end of the board. Using a table-mounted router or table saw, cut away the shaded area on either side of the tenon.

2. Cut away the shaded area directly above and below the tenon. (The view in the third tenon illustration shows the rectangular tenon that is left after completing steps 1 and 2.)

3. Draw an arc on the top and bottom of the tenon that is the same diameter as the width of the tenon. (While our example uses a rounded tenon and mortise, you could leave the tenon as shown and square up the corners of the mortise.)

4. To round the ends of this tenon, use a mallet and wood chisel to cut away the shaded area. Chisel off small amounts of wood until you have nicely rounded ends.

Mortise

1. Pencil mark the exact location of the mortise on your piece of wood.

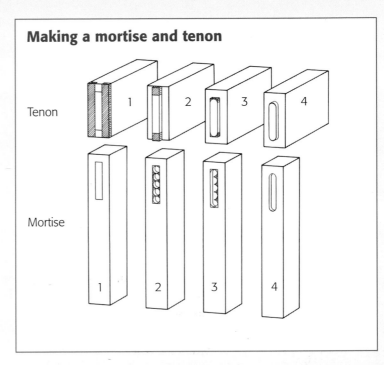

Making a mortise and tenon

Tenon

Mortise

2. Using a drill bit that is the same size as the width of your tenon, drill several holes within the penciled rectangle as shown in the second mortise illustration. Drill each hole to a depth that matches the length of the tenon.

3. With a small chisel and mallet, chisel out the triangular-shaped remnants in the middle of the mortise. After removing all of the unwanted wood from within the mortise, erase or sand off your pencil line. The resulting mortise should accept the matching tenon perfectly.

Space is usually in short supply for avid gardeners. There are so many wonderful plants to grow and so little space to display them. The tiered, semicircular shelves of this Potted Plant Stand offer more than 10 linear ft. of shelf space, while having a footprint of only 2 ft. by 4 ft. A collection of potted plants has plenty of room to grow, and the resulting display makes an attractive pyramidal arrangement.

This Potted Plant Stand will contribute a touch of vintage decor to any sunroom, covered porch, or greenhouse. Use your imagination and bring this versatile piece of furniture indoors during the winter months for displaying houseplants, books, or other collectibles.

This delightful Potted Plant Stand is made from relatively few components. All four plywood shelves are cut from one piece of ¾-in. birch plywood, while the rest of the rails and braces are made

The vintage styling of this Potted Plant Stand makes it an elegant addition to a sunroom, greenhouse, or covered porch.

POTTED PLANT STAND MATERIALS LIST

Key	Qty.	Description	Finished Dimensions	Material
A	1	Lower back rail	¾ in. x 2½ in. x 46 in.	Poplar, pine, or fir
B	1	Middle back rail	¾ in. x 2½ in. x 30 in.	Poplar, pine, or fir
C	1	Upper back rail	¾ in. x 2½ in. x 16 in.	Poplar, pine, or fir
D	1	Upper front rail	¾ in. x 2½ in. x 8 in.	Poplar, pine, or fir
E	1	Middle front rail	¾ in. x 2½ in. x 15 in.	Poplar, pine, or fir
F	1	Lower front rail	¾ in. x 2½ in. x 21 in.	Poplar, pine, or fir
G	2	Front supports	¾ in. x 4 in. x 27¾ in.	Poplar, pine, or fir
H	1	Spacer	¾ in. x 3½ in. x 3¾ in.	Poplar, pine, or fir
I	2	Rear supports	¾ in. x 5 in. x 41 in.	Poplar, pine, or fir
J	2	Middle supports	¾ in. x 1½ in. x 40 in.	Poplar, pine, or fir
K	1	Lower shelf	¾ in. x 24 in. x 48 in.	Birch plywood
L	1	Middle shelf	¾ in. x 16 in. x 32 in.	Birch plywood
M	1	Upper shelf	¾ in. x 9 in. x 18 in.	Birch plywood
N	1	Top shelf	¾ in. x 3 in. x 6 in.	Birch plywood
O	1	Back board	¾ in. x 4¼ in. x 6¼ in.	Poplar, pine, or fir
P	7	Shelf facings	1/16 in. x ¾ in. x various lengths	Cedar
Q	3	Legs	1⅜ in. x 7¾ in.	Commercially made
R	3	Leg-mounting plates	⅜ in. x 2⅜ in. x 2⅜ in.	Steel (includes screws)
S	28	Wood screws	#7 x 1¼ in.	Galvanized
T	19	Wood screws	#8 x 2 in.	Galvanized
U	40	Finishing nails	4d	Galvanized

from standard–size clear wood boards. The legs are commercially made and mount underneath the bottom shelf using available mounting plates. Each leg has a bolt installed in one end that screws into a nut welded in the center of each plate. If the stand will be placed in a greenhouse or other humid area, it's a good idea to spray each plate with a protective coating of paint.

After we applied a primer coat, we finished the stand with a latex semigloss paint. To avoid damaging the wood, we recommend you keep your plant stand out of direct contact with the weather and place waterproof saucers under your potted plants.

1 Cut all of the boards to size, using the top illustration at right to cut out the shelves from a 2-ft. by 4-ft. sheet of plywood. The three grids in the bottom illustration show how to cut out the front supports (G), rear supports (I), and back board (O).

2 Sand all edges of the boards and shelves smooth. We lightly rounded the edges of the support boards with sandpaper to give these four serpentine supports a softer look.

3 Begin assembly by attaching the three back rails (A, B, C) to the three corresponding front rails (D, E, F), as shown in the illustration on p. 82. Use two wood screws (T) at each joint, installing them from the back of the rear rail and driving them into the end of the front rail. As always, predrill and countersink the screw holes to prevent splitting the wood.

4 Place the two middle supports (J) as shown in the illustration on p. 82, and attach them to all three rail assemblies with two wood screws (S) at each joint.

Again, install the screws from the rear of the back rails.

5 Before installing the two front supports (G), temporarily set the shelves (with the exception of the top one) in place. By doing this, you can make sure that these two boards will not interfere with the final placement of the shelves. When the front supports are positioned correctly, clamp them in place and secure them with one wood screw (S) at each joint.

Potted Plant Stand shelf cutting diagram

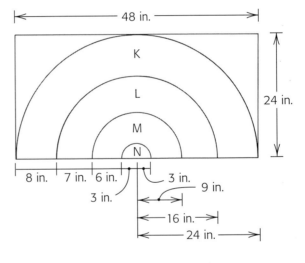

Potted Plant Stand frame grids

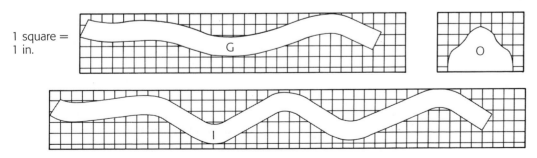

This plant stand is composed of four semicircular shelves supported by a simple frame.

Potted Plant Stand frame assembly

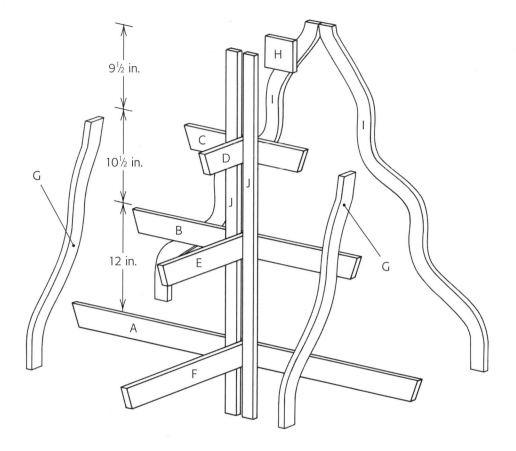

9½ in.

10½ in.

12 in.

G

C

D

H

I

I

J

J

B

E

G

A

F

6 Next, attach the spacer board (H) and two rear supports (I). The spacer board attaches to the back of both middle support boards, as shown in the illustration above. Use two wood screws (S) to secure the spacer, then attach the rear supports. The tops of these two boards should be even with the tops of both the spacer and the middle supports. The bottom end of these boards should be flush with the bottom edge of the lower back rail, just shy of the two ends of that board. Secure the tops of the rear supports to the spacer with one wood screw (T) each. Use one wood screw (S) at each of the remaining six junctions of the rear supports and the back rails. Install these screws from the back of the rear supports.

7 Install all four shelves. The bottom three shelves (K, L, M) are fastened to the rails using three wood screws (T) for each shelf. One screw is driven through each shelf into the front rails, while the other two are driven into the rear rails at both ends of each shelf. The top shelf (N) is fastened to the tops of the rear supports using two screws (T). The back edge of the top shelf is flush with the back edge of the spacer.

8 Attach the back board (O) to the back of the top shelf with two wood screws (S), as shown in the illustration at right.

9 Set the plant stand on its back and attach the three leg mounting plates (R) with the screws provided in the package. The front leg plate fastens directly in front of the lower front rail, while the other two leg plates attach to the under-side of the lower shelf near the ends of the lower back rail (see the illustration at right). Once the plates are secured, screw in all three legs (Q) until they are tight, and set the stand upright.

10 The last step before painting is optional. We decided to add a thin fac-ing strip (P) to the front of the shelves to conceal the plywood edges. We ripped the facing strips from a length of 3/4–in. cedar board. Because the strips are only 1/16 in. thick, they easily followed the curve of the bottom three shelves. The top shelf has a radius that is too small to successfully attach these thin strips, so we carefully sanded and filled this edge before painting.

To attach each facing strip, apply a thin coat of wood glue along the entire edge of the shelf. Starting at one end, attach the facing strip to the edge of the shelf with 4d finishing nails (U) every 4 in. to 6 in. Countersink the nails so the holes can be filled, then allow the glue to dry before trimming off any excess. Next, fill all the nail and screw holes in the plant stand, as well as any gaps between the facing strips and shelves. Sand the entire stand and finish as desired.

Potted Plant Stand assembly of shelves and legs

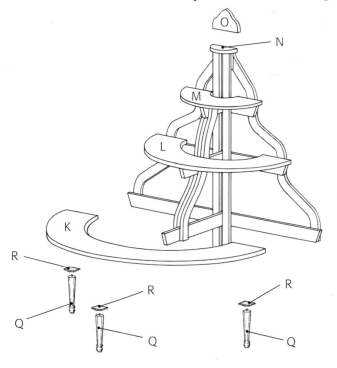

The turned legs add to the plant stand's charm yet are inexpensive and can be found at most home centers.

For most gardeners, there is no greater treat than harvesting fresh homegrown vegetables. But cleaning and preparing them in your kitchen can leave behind a mess of soil, grit, debris, and insects. To combat this problem, many home growers resort to building an outdoor washstand.

Conveniently located near the compost bin, our Vegetable Washstand has a variety of uses. Its obvious use is for washing and preparing vegetables, but it's also perfect for outdoor entertaining, flower arranging, and washing muddy garden hands. For easy access, the cupboard space beneath the sink stores a harvesting basket, tools, a cutting board, and cups for cold drinking water on hot summer days. This all-purpose outdoor sink will keep your kitchen clean and the soil and bugs in the garden where they belong.

If you grow vegetables, arrange flowers, or entertain outdoors, this Vegetable Washstand will be used all summer long.

VEGETABLE WASHSTAND MATERIALS LIST

Key	Qty.	Description	Finished Dimensions	Material
A	4	End frame boards	1½ in. x 3½ in. x 30 in.	Treated lumber
B	4	End frame boards	1½ in. x 3½ in. x 22¾ in.	Treated lumber
C	2	End frame boards	1½ in. x 7½ in. x 19¾ in.	Treated lumber
D	4	Middle frame boards	1½ in. x 3½ in. x 47¼ in.	Treated lumber
E	6	Middle frame boards	1½ in. x 3½ in. x 31½ in.	Treated lumber
F	2	Top frame boards	1½ in. x 3½ in. x 19¾ in.	Treated lumber
G	1	Wood countertop	¾ in. x 28¾ in. x 60¼ in.	ABX plywood
H	28	Siding boards	¾ in. x 5⅜ in. x 33½ in.	Cedar (T&G siding)
I	2	Trim boards	¾ in. x 3½ in. x 57¼ in.	Cedar
J	2	Trim boards	¾ in. x 2 in. x 57¼ in.	Cedar
K	10	Trim boards	¾ in. x 3½ in. x 28 in.	Cedar
L	2	Trim boards	¾ in. x 3½ in. x 24¼ in.	Cedar
M	2	Trim boards	¾ in. x 2 in. x 24¼ in.	Cedar
N	8	Door boards	¾ in. x 5⅜ in. x 27¾ in.	Cedar (T&G siding)
O	4	Door trim	¾ in. x 3½ in. x 16⅜ in.	Cedar
P	4	Door trim	¾ in. x 3½ in. x 20⅜ in.	Cedar
Q	2	Door stops	¾ in. x 1½ in. x 33¼ in.	Cedar
R	2	Door stops	¾ in. x 1½ in. x 26½ in.	Cedar
S	6	Concrete	60-lb. bag (½ cu. ft.)	Premix concrete
T	4	Carriage bolts	⅜ in. x 5 in.	Galvanized
U	4	Washers	⅜ in.	Galvanized
V	4	Nuts	⅜ in.	Galvanized
W	1	Waterline	Custom installed	Galvanized pipe
X	1	Drainline	4 in.	PVC pipe
Y	1	Metal countertop	1¾ in. x 28¾ in. x 60¼ in.	Stainless steel
Z	1	Sink	22 in. x 25 in. x 6½ in.	Stainless steel
AA	1	Faucet	To fit sink	Plated brass

VEGETABLE WASHSTAND MATERIALS LIST continued

BB*	4	Hinges	2 in. to 3 in.	Painted, brass, or stainless steel
CC*	2	Handles	3 in. to 4 in.	Painted, brass, or stainless steel
DD*	1	Hook & eye	3 in. to 4 in.	Painted, brass, or stainless steel
EE	52	Box nails	10d	Galvanized
FF	4	L-brackets	1½ in.	Galvanized
GG*	70	Wood screws	#8 x 2 in.	Galvanized
HH*	74	Wood screws	#8 x 2 in.	Stainless steel
II*	24	Wood screws	#7 x 1¼ in.	Stainless steel

*See project resources on p. 179.

Quantities listed for screws and nails are approximations.

Designing this Vegetable Washstand presented us with a few interesting challenges: It had to be sturdy, weather-proof, and easily accessible. Here in the Pacific Northwest, we often experience the rain this part of the country has a reputation for, so we knew the material we used for the countertop would have to stand up to water. After talking to a local sheet-metal fabricator, we decided on stainless steel as the best option. We asked about using galvanized sheet metal, but he pointed out that the inevitable scratches to the surface would eventually rust. Copy the pattern at right and bring it with you to obtain estimates from sheet-metal fabricators in your area. When you decide on a shop to make the countertop, leave a copy of the pattern with them for reference.

To make the washstand resistant to high winds, we decided to build it on top of a small concrete slab, which gave it a great deal of stability. The internal frame is made of treated lumber, while the siding is cut from standard tongue-

Vegetable Washstand countertop template

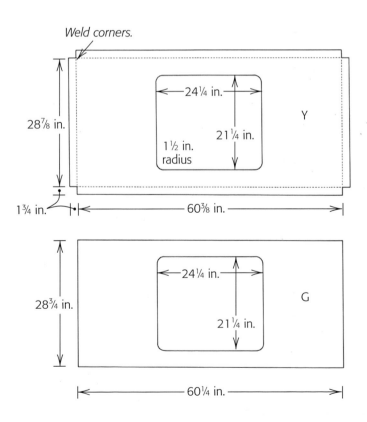

Check your local permit and code requirements before you install the plumbing.

The side spigot is handy for filling a watering can or attaching a hose.

Vegetable Washstand plumbing assembly

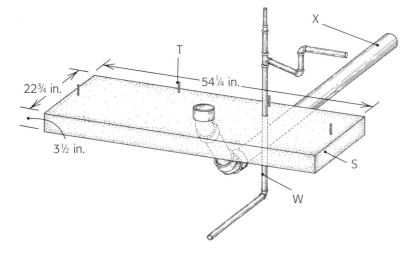

22¾ in.

54¼ in.

3½ in.

X

T

S

W

and–groove cedar. To ensure longevity, we covered the siding and trim boards with a semitransparent, oil–based stain. The combination of a stainless steel countertop and wood–framed cabinet will hold up equally well in colder climates. Each fall, drain the incoming waterline to prevent the pipes from freezing. This sink will be able to withstand the elements like an outdoor shed, but if you're concerned about winter damage, you could also cover the washstand with a waterproof tarp.

1 Before you begin mixing cement to create the footing, determine how you are going to hook up your waterline and drain system. In the following illustrations and photos, we show you how our system is hooked up, but you may want to check with your local municipality for specific rules concerning these hookups. Also, if you are not comfortable doing your own plumbing work, consult a professional for this part of the construction.

From an existing waterline, we ran ¾-in. galvanized pipe (W) into the washstand, as shown in the illustration on the facing page. We created a T–joint to facilitate an outside spigot in addition to the main waterline. Above the T–joint, we reduced the ¾-in. pipe to ½ in., which provides a standard connection for the faucet feed tube. Not pictured is an in–ground cutoff valve that allows us to turn the water off in the winter. If you live in a particularly cold climate, you may want to install a bleeder valve to completely empty the pipes each winter.

The drain consists of 4–in. PVC pipe (X) that carries the water from inside the washstand to a simple drywell about 10 ft. behind the stand. The drywell consists of a hole about 4 ft. deep and 2 ft. in diameter filled with small stones and gravel. Because we have sandy soil, this has proven to be more than adequate. If your soil is mostly clay, you might want to make a larger well. However, for the volume of water that is normally used for vegetables, a large well is probably unnecessary. Install the waterline and drain before pouring your foundation.

2 Make a simple foundation form out of scrap 2x4s to create the slab shown in the illustration on the facing page. You will need about six bags of premix concrete (S). As you pour in the concrete, install the carriage bolts (T). With a trowel, work the concrete around the water and drain pipes and smooth the surface. Let the concrete set overnight before removing the forms, then allow the concrete to cure for a few days before building the frame.

3 After cutting all the wood boards to size, nail together the two end frames, which are comprised of end frame boards (A, B, C), using box nails (EE) (see the illustration below). Mark the position of the carriage bolts on the bottom of each end frame, then drill ⅝-in. holes to accept the bolts. Set the frames in position and thumb–tighten the nuts and washers (U, V). If you decided to plumb in an outside spigot, you will also need to drill an appropriate size hole in board (C).

4 Next, build the two middle frames using boards (D, E) with box nails (EE), as shown in the illustration on p. 90. Notice that the top board of each middle frame is placed vertically into notches cut in boards (E). You will also need to cut four notches along the top edges of the frame that will later allow room for the sink clamps.

Vegetable Washstand end wall frame assembly

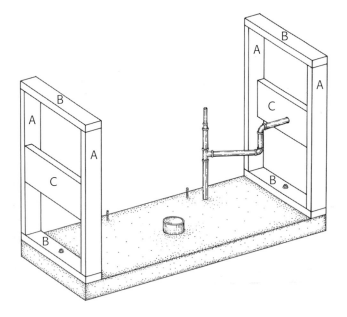

Vegetable Washstand front and back frame assembly

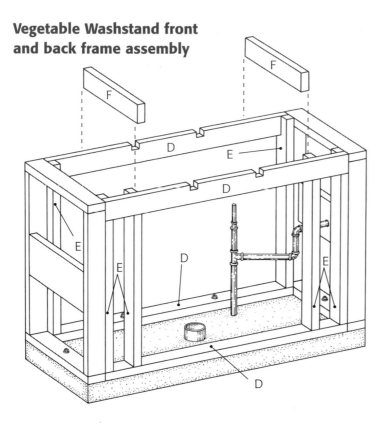

5 Nail the two top frame boards (F) in place with box nails (EE), as shown in the illustration above.

6 With the basic frame complete, combine the wood countertop (G), metal countertop (Y), and the sink (Z). First set the wood countertop on the frame and adjust its position to overhang the frame 3 in. on all sides. Draw a pencil line where the frame meets the underside of the countertop for reference. Then set the metal countertop and sink in place, as shown in the illustration on the facing page. To seal the sink opening from rain, apply a layer or two of ¼-in.-thick closed-cell foam or use glazing tape around the edge of the opening.

7 With the sink set in place, use the supplied clamps to secure it to the countertops. Position four of the clamps to sit in the notched spaces along the top edges of the middle frames. Because the wood countertop is still unattached, you can move it around to make mounting the sink easier.

8 Next, secure the wood countertop to the frame with four L-brackets (FF) using the screws provided. Attach the brackets from underneath the countertop along the top frame boards (F). These brackets hold the countertop securely to the frame, while still allowing you to remove it if necessary.

9 Install the cedar siding (H) using the top illustration on p. 92 as a guide. Notice that the trim boards completely cover the corners so a perfect matchup is not necessary. You will need to rip the siding that borders the door opening (on the left and right) to eliminate either the tongue or groove. Since you will need to cut the siding from standard lengths, there should be plenty of cut-offs from which to make the pieces above and below the door opening. These small pieces act as spacers and are covered by the trim boards. Attach all of the cedar siding with wood screws (GG). Use one screw at the top and one at the bottom of each board. Use one screw to attach each of the spacer boards. We used the less expensive galvanized screws to secure the cedar siding because the trim boards will cover them.

10 Secure all of the final trim boards (I thru M) with the stainless steel screws (HH), using the top illustration on p. 92

as a guide. Use three to five wood screws per board depending on the length.

11 Next, put in the door stops (Q, R). These are cut from cedar 1x2s and are secured with three wood screws (HH) per board.

12 Before the front doors are assembled and attached, apply a protective finish to your washstand.

13 To match the rest of the washstand, make the two front doors from tongue–and–groove siding combined with front trim boards of 1x4 cedar (see the bottom illustration on p. 92). The trim boards (O, P) lock the tongue–and–groove cedar boards (N) together. Use about 12 wood screws (II) per door, driving each screw from the back side of the door. Once the doors are assembled, apply the same protective finish to the doors that you applied to the rest of the

Vegetable Washstand sink and countertop assembly

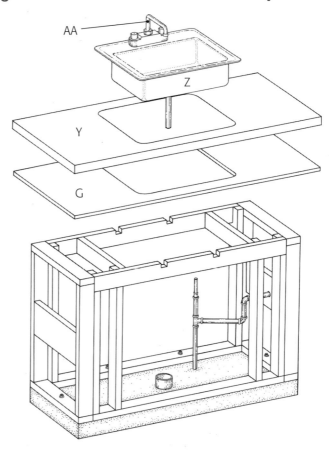

Conveniently located near the vegetable garden and compost bin, this washstand allows you to leave bugs, grit, and debris outdoors.

Vegetable Washstand siding and trim boards assembly

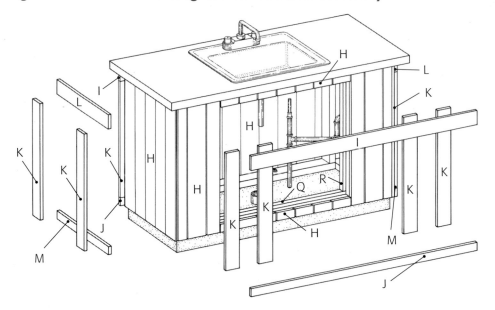

Vegetable Washstand cabinet door assembly

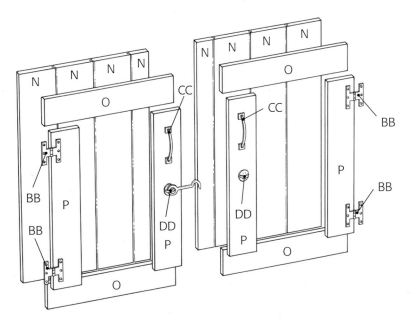

washstand. Next, add the hinges and handles (BB, CC) to the front of both doors. These can be almost any style but should be painted or made from a weather-resistant material. Mount the doors to the front of the washstand and check them for free movement. Add the hook-and-eye latch (DD) after the doors are hung.

14 Finally, add a faucet (AA) to your sink. When choosing a faucet style, look for one with an extended, high spout to allow enough room for a large head of cabbage. After tightening the locking nuts on the underside of the sink, hook one end of a flexible water-supply hose to the cold water end of the faucet and the other to the incoming water supply. You will also need to buy a drainpipe extension to direct the rinse water into the PVC drain opening (see the photo at left on p. 88). With everything hooked up and ready to go, you'll be ready to enjoy the convenience of having a wash area right near the garden.

The stainless steel countertop and cedar tongue-and-groove cabinet make this unit weather resistant.

Structures for Growing Plants

In nature, only the plants best suited for a particular environment will thrive. But over the centuries we have learned to artificially simulate special conditions to grow plants in areas where they are not indigenous. This chapter shows you how to build garden structures that allow us to "adjust" nature. If, for example, your region is plagued with clay or rocky soil, consider building a Raised Bed. If you live in an area with a short growing season, perhaps a Cold Frame or Greenhouse will give your garden a head start. Or, if you long for slug-free strawberries, consider building a Strawberry Tower.

Gardening in raised beds has so many advantages that it's difficult to name many disadvantages. The simple yet elegant lines of this Raised Bed will help you grow a variety of plants and at the same time visually enhance your landscape. Raised beds are ideal for gardeners living in regions of poor soil. Filled with a combination of topsoil, compost, aged manure, and peat moss, a raised bed will produce lush crops of flowers and vegetables. The improved raised soil will drain freely and warm quickly in the spring for earlier planting.

Raised beds can also be used as mini-nurseries where newly rooted cuttings can grow until they're ready for transplanting to their permanent positions in the garden. Similarly, you can grow new varieties in a raised bed so you can observe their growth habits and colors before strategically placing them in a coordinated landscape.

Enhance the growth of flowers and vegetables in this attractive Raised Bed.

RAISED BED MATERIALS LIST

Key	Qty.	Description	Finished Dimensions	Material
A	4	Corner posts	3½ in. x 3½ in. x 24 in.	Cedar
B	2	Upper side frame boards	1½ in. x 5½ in. x 78 in.	Cedar
C	2	Lower side frame boards	1½ in. x 5½ in. x 78 in.	Cedar
D	2	Upper end frame boards	1½ in. x 5½ in. x 54 in.	Cedar
E	2	Lower end frame boards	1½ in. x 5½ in. x 54 in.	Cedar
F	8	Tie boards	¾ in. x 1½ in. x 9 in.	Cedar
G	16	Lag screws	¼ in. x 5 in.	Galvanized
H	16	Dowel plugs	¾ in. x ½ in.	Hardwood
I	16	Washers	¼ in. (I.D.)	Galvanized
J	32	Wood screws	#8 x 2 in.	Galvanized

Although advantages far outweigh the disadvantages, it's worth mentioning that the plants in your raised bed may need extra water due to the free-draining soil. Also, if your region experiences extremely cold weather, the elevated soil may freeze sooner and to a greater depth.

Depending on your needs, you can build one raised bed or several. If you construct more than one, reduce weeds and early spring mud by installing permanent paths between the beds. Materials such as gravel, bark chips, and paving stones work well. The narrow design of this raised bed allows easy access to the entire growing area, and its sturdy construction will give years of enjoyment.

While raised beds are a fairly common sight in backyard gardens, we wanted to design a raised bed that added a little more architectural detail to the basic frame. Another goal was to minimize the "cupping" of the perimeter boards that plagues many of the raised beds we have seen. To do this, we cut two "plough" grooves in two adjacent faces of each post to accept the perimeter frame boards. These grooves (a type of open mortise) prevent the 2x6 frame boards from cupping due to moisture. The corner posts also have a shallow pointed top and a circumference groove to add interest.

1 After cutting all the boards to size, begin by making the shallow end points on the tops of the four corner posts (A). To do this, set the miter gauge on your table saw to make a 30° cut and pass each corner post through the saw four times. The blade should contact the end of the post in the very middle, cutting at an angle toward the side of the post (see the illustration on the facing page).

2 After you have cut the top points, set the sawblade to a height of ½ in. and cut the ½-in.-wide circumference groove around each post, starting the groove 4 in. from the top of the post. Unless you use a dado blade set to cut a width of ½ in., you will need to make four or five passes through the saw for each side.

3 To finish shaping the end posts, make the two plough grooves on two adjacent sides of each post. These grooves will accept the side and end frame boards and will help prevent them from cupping. Pencil mark the position of each plough groove before you begin (see the illustration at right). Then, using a 1½-in. wood drill bit, drill a hole 1½ in. in diameter and ½ in. deep. The top of this hole is 1½ in. below the bottom edge of the circumference groove, or 6 in. from the top of the post.

Make two additional holes just below and overlapping the top one, then chisel away the triangular remnants of wood that remain between the holes. You should be left with an elongated oval hole that is ½ in. deep. This elongated hole enables you to use your table saw to complete the plough groove.

With your sawblade still set to a height of ½ in., move the rip fence 1 in. from the sawblade. Starting at the bottom of the post, pass the post through the blade until the blade reaches the bottom hole that was drilled. Be careful not to push the post too far or the sawblade may contact the area above the top hole. Repeat this step several times, moving the rip fence away from the blade in ⅛-in. increments until the entire plough groove has been cut. Create the grooves in the remaining three posts in the same way.

Decorative end posts keep the side walls of the Raised Bed straight and well anchored.

Raised Bed end post profile

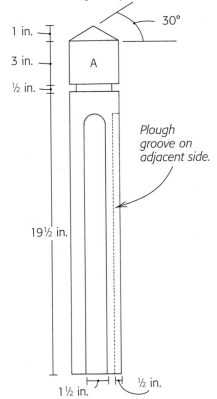

1 in.

3 in.

A

30°

½ in.

Plough groove on adjacent side.

19½ in.

1½ in.

½ in.

4 Next, build the side and end frame sections by combining two boards for each side section (see the illustration at left below). The top 2x6 boards (B, D) on each side are notched and shaped to match the top of the plough groove on the post. To do this, cut the notch with a backsaw and shape the tenon with a chisel. When the frame sections are inserted into the plough grooves, it leaves a nice clean joint at the top of each junction.

5 When all of the top frame boards are complete, combine them with the two lower side and end frame boards (C, E) using the 9-in. tie boards (F). Attach each tie with four wood screws (J), two screws in each frame board (see the illustration at right below). These ties won't show once you fill the raised bed with dirt.

6 Before attaching the frame sections to the posts, apply any stain or preservative/sealer you may want to use. Since the raised bed will likely be used for vegetable crops, read the label on the can to make sure the finish is nontoxic when completely cured.

7 Assemble the raised bed frame by attaching two end posts to both ends of the two side frame sections (see the top illustration on the facing page). On the outside edge of each post, opposite the side frame sections, drill two ¾-in. holes about 1 in. deep, as shown in the bottom illustration on the facing page. Slightly offset these holes from the middle of each board. Then, in the center of each hole, drill a ¼-in. pilot hole that is about 5½ in. deep from the surface of the post for the 5-in. lag screws (G). Slip a washer (I) onto each lag screw and install them into each pilot hole. When you're finished, all four corner posts should be attached to either end of the side frame sections.

Raised Bed side and end wall assembly

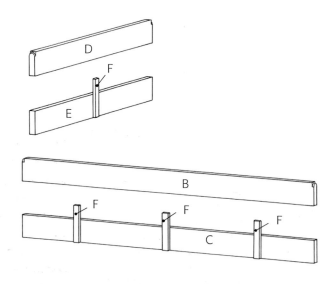

Closeup of Raised Bed wall construction

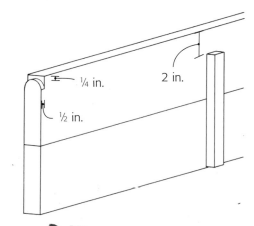

Raised Bed assembly

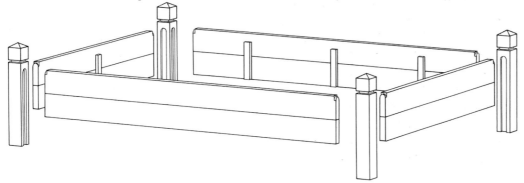

8 Repeat these same steps to secure the end frame sections to the same four posts. Once the raised bed is assembled, cut 16 dowel plugs (H) from a length of ¾-in. hardwood dowel. With a little glue, insert these plugs into the four holes on each corner post until they are flush with the surface.

9 When you move the raised bed to your desired site in the garden, mark the ground where the four posts sit, then set the raised bed aside. At each mark, excavate holes about 7 in. deep, then set the raised bed back in place with the posts sitting in the holes. Level the raised bed by adding dirt to the holes if necessary. By putting the corner posts partially in the ground, the raised bed is sturdier and less prone to being pushed out of shape.

If you have applied a finish to the wood, make sure it sits empty for a week or two to ensure that it has cured. Then fill the bed with a good mixture of soil, peat moss, aged manure, and other amendments you may deem necessary. The only thing left to do is to fill it with your favorite flowers or vegetables in the spring!

Raised Bed lag screw attachment

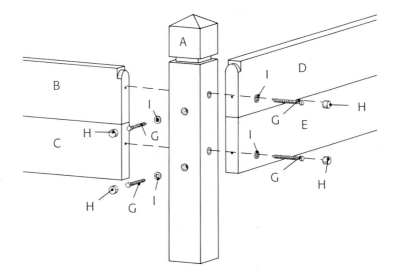

Raised beds are perfect for growing vegetables, flowers, newly rooted cuttings, and biennials that will be transplanted to your garden the following year.

COLD FRAME

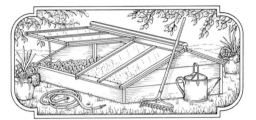

If you grow your own seedlings, a cold frame is an essential part of spring planting. In cold regions, it allows you to get a head start on the growing season by protecting young plants from chilly spring weather. A cold frame can be easily constructed from PVC pipes and plastic sheeting, but this type of structure does nothing to enhance the landscape. This Cold Frame, on the other hand, is reminiscent of frames used in the late 19th century. Based on historic designs, this sturdy Cold Frame will add a bit of classic garden architecture to your yard.

Once your frame is finished, we suggest you cover the dirt floor with landscape fabric to reduce weeds, topped with a layer of pea gravel for proper drainage. Because mud is such an integral part of spring, we also suggest surrounding your cold frame with a path of gravel or paving stones. This not only provides dry footing but also discour-

If you grow your own seedlings, a Cold Frame is indispensable in early spring.

COLD FRAME MATERIALS LIST

Key	Qty.	Description	Finished Dimensions	Material
Cold Frame				
A	3	Side frame boards	1½ in. x 7½ in. x 84 in.	Cedar
B	2	End frame boards	1½ in. x 7½ in. x 39¾ in.	Cedar
C	2	End frame boards	1½ in. x 7½ in. x 57 in.	Cedar
D	2	End frame boards	1½ in. x 7½ in. x 57 in.	Cedar
E	2	End tie boards	1½ in. x 1½ in. x 20 in.	Cedar
F	2	End tie boards	1½ in. x 1½ in. x 15½ in.	Cedar
G	2	End tie boards	1½ in. x 1½ in. x 8⅛ in.	Cedar
H	1	Side tie board	1½ in. x 1½ in. x 13⅛ in.	Cedar
I	1	Side tie board	1½ in. x 1½ in. x 5⅝ in.	Cedar
J	1	Ridge board	1½ in. x 5½ in. x 84 in.	Cedar
K	1	Ridge cap	1½ in. x 3½ in. x 84 in.	Cedar
L	1	Window support	1½ in. x 2¼ in. x 39⅝ in.	Cedar
M	1	Window support	1½ in. x 2¼ in. x 24¼ in.	Cedar
N	60	Wood screws	#8 x 2½ in.	Galvanized or stainless steel
Windows				
O	4	Top frame boards	¾ in. x 3 in. x 37½ in.	Cedar
P	4	Bottom frame boards	¾ in. x 3½ in. x 37½ in.	Cedar
Q	2	Large middle frame boards	¾ in. x 2½ in. x 33½ in.	Cedar
R	2	Small middle frame boards	¾ in. x 2½ in. x 18½ in.	Cedar
S	4	Large side frame boards	¾ in. x 2½ in. x 40 in.	Cedar
T	4	Small side frame boards	¾ in. x 2½ in. x 25 in.	Cedar
U	4	Top retainer boards	¾ in. x 3⅜ in. x 42½ in.	Cedar
V	2	Large middle retainer boards	¾ in. x 2½ in. x 37 in.	Cedar
W	2	Small middle retainer boards	¾ in. x 2½ in. x 22 in.	Cedar
X	4	Large side retainer boards	¾ in. x 2½ in. x 37 in.	Cedar

COLD FRAME MATERIALS LIST continued

Y	4	Small side retainer boards	¾ in. x 2½ in. x 22 in.	Cedar
Z	8	Plugs	³⁄₁₆ in. x ⅜ in. x ¾ in.	Cedar
AA*	48	Dowel pins	¼ in. x 2 in.	Hardwood
BB	4	Large window glass	¹⁄₁₆ in. x 18 in. x 34¼ in.	Window glass
CC	4	Small window glass	¹⁄₁₆ in. x 18 in. x 19¼ in.	Window glass
DD*	1	Glazing tape	⅛ in. x ⅜ in. x 48 ft.	Closed-cell foam
EE	16	Escutcheon pins	18 in. x ¾ in.	Brass
FF*	8	Hinges	2 in. x 2 in.	Stainless steel or brass
GG*	52	Wood screws	#6 x 1¼ in.	Stainless steel
HH	4	Dowel rods	¾ in. x 48 in.	Hardwood

*See project resources on p. 179.

ages slugs from entering the frame. The generous 5-ft. by 7-ft. dimension of the Cold Frame accommodates numerous potted plants or 17 standard 11-in. by 22-in. seedling flats. Whether you use a cold frame for starting spring seedlings, forcing bulbs, or overwintering half-hardy plants, this frame will help you garden in a style that has lasted for decades.

The frame and windows of this Cold Frame are classically designed and relatively easy to build. The glass panes sit on a simple doweled window frame, held in place by a set of retaining boards and foam glazing tape. Each separate window frame has a bevel cut at the top end to match the pitch of the windows. The lower frame is mainly constructed of 2x8 cedar boards held together with 2x2 cedar ties. Along the top of the ridge board, we've added a ridge cap to help keep the rain out.

The large front windows and the smaller rear ones open wide for easy access.

Cold Frame walls and ridge assembly

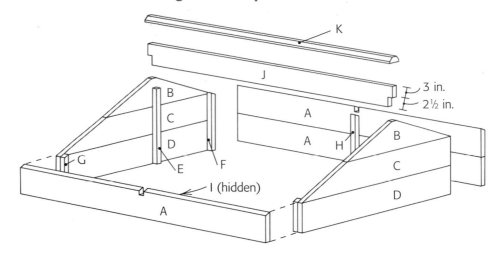

Cold Frame end wall profile

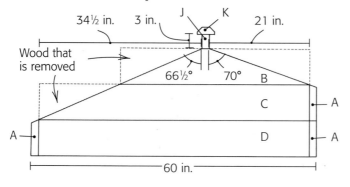

FRAME

1 Cut all of the frame boards to size. You may want to leave the top board (B) of the two end frames cut a little full (to 40 in.). By doing this, you can still cut the top (B) and middle (C) board out of one 2x8.

2 On a flat surface, butt the three end boards (B, C, D) together, as shown in the illustration at left. Align the three back edges of these boards. On what will be the interior surface of the end wall, attach the end tie board (E) with six wood screws (N). Drive two screws through the end tie board into each of the three end wall boards to lock them together, as shown in the illustration above. Repeat this step for the opposite end wall.

3 Place one of the end walls on a set of sawhorses with the end tie board facing down. Make two pencil marks on the top edge of board (B) indicating

While the Cold Frame can sit directly on the ground, we decided to set ours on a footing of treated 4x4s to help prolong the life of the lower frame boards. This also gave us a little more headroom inside the frame. Another option you may want to consider is the addition of automatic lifters for the rear set of windows. By using these solar-powered lifters, you don't have to constantly monitor the cold frame in changing weather conditions.

where the ridge board will sit. With a straightedge, draw a pencil line from the rear pencil mark to the top rear corner of board (C). This creates the correct pitch for the smaller rear windows. Then use the straightedge to draw a pencil line from the front pencil mark to the top front corner of board (D), which marks the correct pitch for the larger front windows. Using a circular saw and a straightedge, cut along the pencil marks to create the end wall profile shown in the bottom illustration on the facing page. Repeat this step for the opposite end wall.

4 Cut the end tie boards (F, G) to the correct length and angle by holding the boards in position on the end wall and pencil marking the exact location of the cuts. Attach the end tie boards with four wood screws (N) for boards (F) and two screws for boards (G).

5 Complete the end walls by driving a wood screw (N) into each of the tapered joints in each end wall. For each end wall, drive one screw through the tapered end of board (C) into board (D), and drive two more through both tapered ends of board (B) into board (C).

6 Prepare the two boards that make up the rear wall of the frame and the one used for the front. All three of these boards (A) are the same length, but their top edges are different. On the single front wall board, cut a 66½° bevel along the top edge, as shown in the bottom illustration on the facing page. For the rear wall, cut the upper board to a 70° bevel to match the pitch of the rear windows. The lower board is not beveled. Before attaching the front and rear frame boards to the end walls, create a notch in the center of the front board and in the upper rear board. Cut each 1½-in.-wide notch to a depth of 1 in. below the bottom edge of each bevel. These notches will later accept the ends of the window support boards.

7 Attach the side frame boards to the end walls with three wood screws (N) at the end of each side frame board (A). Two screws anchor into the end walls and one into either tie board (F) or (G).

Cold Frame grooved window support board assembly

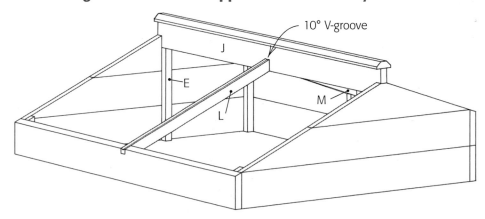

10° V-groove

The supports between the windows are grooved to channel rainwater away.

Cold Frame window support board profile

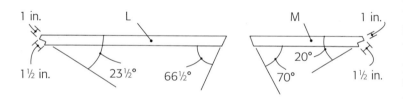

1 in.   L   M   1 in.

1½ in.   23½°   66½°   20°   70°   1½ in.

8 Notch the ends of the ridge board (J) and set it in place, as shown in the illustration on p. 107. The bottom of the ridge board should rest on the tops of end tie boards (E). Secure the ridge board by driving two wood screws (N) through the ends of the end walls.

9 Next, cut the two window support boards (L, M) to size, as shown in the illustration above. The top edges of both boards have a 10° V–cut running the length of the boards. This channel collects rainwater that seeps between the windows and empties it to the outside

of the frame (for a view of this channel, see the photo at left). You can create this channel on a table saw by setting the blade to a 10° tilt and a height of ¾ in. Set the rip fence 2¼ in. from the base of the blade and run each board through once, flip it over, and run it through again.

10 Set one end of each window support board into the notch cut in the side frame board. The other end should butt up against the ridge board, as shown in the illustration on p. 107. Anchor each window support board by driving one screw through the notched end of each board into the side frame board. At the other end, drive one screw on either side of each board at an angle into the ridge board.

11 With the window support boards in place, pencil mark and cut the last two tie boards (H, I) that sit directly below the window support boards. These tie boards brace the window support boards and, in the case of tie board (H), connect the two rear side boards in the middle of the frame. Use two wood screws (N) to attach the front tie board (I) and four screws to attach the rear tie board (H).

12 Finally, attach the ridge cap board (K). The ridge cap is made from a standard cedar 2x4. Cut two 45° bevels on the top of the board, as shown in the top illustration on p. 106, then attach it to the top of the ridge board with six evenly spaced wood screws (N).

13 Before you begin the four cold frame windows, apply a protective finish to the frame. We used an oil–based, solid–color stain on ours.

WINDOWS

1 Cut all of the window boards to size. All four windows used in this cold frame have the same width; the difference between the front and back sets of windows is the length.

2 Before making the bottom frames for both sets of windows, cut the chamfers (or bevels) that will run along the top edges of each window. The front windows use a $66\frac{1}{2}°$ chamfer, while the back windows are cut at 70°. Make these bevel cuts along the top edges of boards (O) and (S) for the front windows and along boards (O) and (T) for the back windows (see the profile chart below and the illustration on p. 110).

3 Once the chamfers are cut, begin assembling the window frames. Each frame is joined using hardwood dowels

Cold Frame general window frame assembly

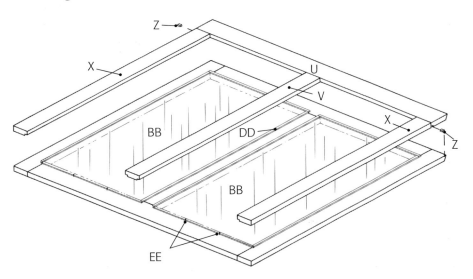

Cold Frame profile chart

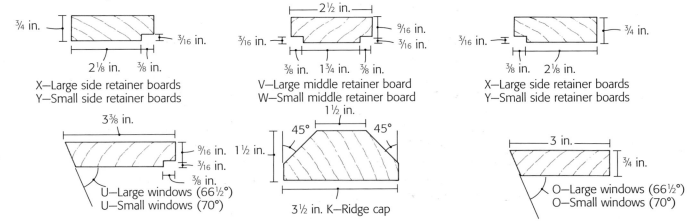

Cold Frame individual frame assembly

BACK WINDOWS

FRONT WINDOWS

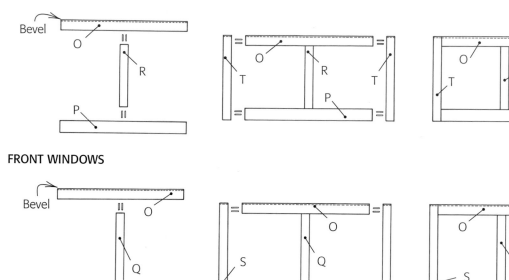

(AA), which create a strong, permanent joint. You will need a doweling jig to accurately place the holes for each dowel (see the sidebar on p. 63). Connect the window frame pieces (O, P, Q, R, S, T) in the order shown in the illustration above. Once each frame is assembled, set it aside to dry for at least 24 hours before continuing. If available, use pipe clamps to hold the pieces of the frame together while the glue, which should be waterproof, sets.

4 Next, prepare the top retaining boards that will hold the glass in place. Notice that the four top retainer boards (U) are chamfered just like the top frame boards. The two that will be used on the front windows have a 66½° bevel, and

the two that will be used on the rear windows have a 70° bevel. There is also a consistent ³⁄₁₆-in. by ³⁄₈-in. rabbet on all the retainer boards. Use the profiles in the bottom illustration on p. 109 to determine where to make the rabbets on these boards. The rabbets provide just enough of a channel to securely hold the glass and the glazing tape. When the retaining boards (U, V, W, X, Y) have been cut, place them on the lower frame for a test fit, then apply the same finish to the window boards that you used on the rest of the cold frame.

5 Cut to size the window glass for the four windows (BB, CC). For instructions on how we cut glass, see the sidebar on pp. 140–141.

6 Tap in two brass escutcheon pins (EE) ½ in. below each window opening, as shown in the top illustration on p. 109. Leave about ⅛ in. of the shank above the board.

7 Set both pieces of glass for each window against the escutcheon pin shanks. The sides and top of each pane should overlap the frame opening by about ¼ in.

8 Apply glazing tape (DD) along the sides and top of each piece of glass. The inside edge of the glazing tape follows the edge of the opening, while the outside edge overhangs the glass by about ⅛ in.

9 With the glass and glazing tape in place, install the retaining boards, as shown in the top illustration on p. 109. Use four wood screws (GG) each to secure retainer boards (U, X, V) and three wood screws (GG) each to secure retainer boards (W, Y). For each window, cut and insert two small cedar plugs (Z) into the rabbets on either side of the window frame.

10 Place the windows on the completed frame. Center the gap between the set of front windows and rear windows directly over the middle of the window support boards (see the illustration below). The two sets of windows should overhang the cold frame by ½ in. on the front, rear, and sides. When all four windows are in place, attach the hinges (FF) as shown.

11 Cut and finish hardwood dowel rods (HH) to be used to hold the windows open. To help the dowel rods stay in place, drill a ⅞-in. hole into the underside of each window frame to accept the rods. The dowel rods can be cut to whatever height you choose for each window.

Locating the cold frame in the garden is your last task. Ideally, you should face the cold frame south so the greatest amount of sunlight can penetrate the front windows. Fortunately, with windows on either side of the center ridge, this frame will catch a good amount of sun in almost any open location.

Cold Frame window hinge attachment

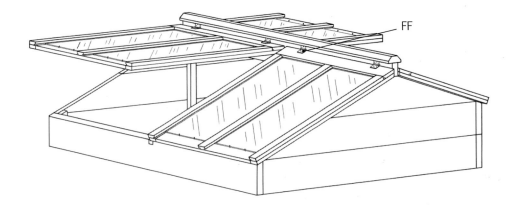

FF

When June arrives, fresh ripe strawberries are the prize of the garden.
Unfortunately, slugs find them just as
tempting and often get to them first.
This Strawberry Tower, however, keeps
the berries well above the ground and
reduces the damage done by these per-
sistent marauders. At the same time, it's
an attractive garden centerpiece that
saves valuable space. By utilizing its vertical growing area, the tower can accommodate up to 90 strawberry plants. If
grown in traditional rows, this number
of plants would consume 60 ft. of row
space. Also, traditional rows often
become choked with runners and young
plants, whereas on the tower, runners
can be easily snipped off as they appear.
If 90 strawberry plants are too many for
your family's needs, consider growing
them on two sides of the tower and
planting the alternate sides with flower-
ing annuals such as alyssum, lobelia,
pansies, and petunias. By midsummer

Standing tall among low-growing veg-etables, this Strawberry Tower is both decora-tive and functional.

STRAWBERRY TOWER MATERIALS LIST

Key	Qty.	Description	Finished Dimensions	Material
A	1	Center post	3½ in. x 3½ in. x 72 in.	Cedar
B	4	Bottom frame boards	¾ in. x 3½ in. x 18 in.	Cedar
C	4	Side frame boards	¾ in. x 3½ in. x 63⅛ in.	Cedar
D	4	Bottom trim boards	¾ in. x 3½ in. x 27½ in.	Cedar
E	4	Soil-retaining boards	¾ in. x 3½ in. x 25¾ in.	Cedar
F	4	Soil-retaining boards	¾ in. x 3½ in. x 24 in.	Cedar
G	4	Soil-retaining boards	¾ in. x 3½ in. x 22¼ in.	Cedar
H	4	Soil-retaining boards	¾ in. x 3½ in. x 20¼ in.	Cedar
I	4	Soil-retaining boards	¾ in. x 3½ in. x 18½ in.	Cedar
J	4	Soil-retaining boards	¾ in. x 3½ in. x 16½ in.	Cedar
K	4	Soil-retaining boards	¾ in. x 3½ in. x 14¾ in.	Cedar
L	4	Soil-retaining boards	¾ in. x 3½ in. x 13 in.	Cedar
M	4	Soil-retaining boards	¾ in. x 3½ in. x 11 in.	Cedar
N	4	Soil-retaining boards	¾ in. x 3½ in. x 9¼ in.	Cedar
O	4	Top trim	¾ in. x 1½ in. x 6½ in.	Cedar
P*	24	Dowel pins	¼ in. x 2½ in.	Hardwood
Q	8	Finishing nails	4d	Galvanized
R*	176	Wood screws	#7 x 1¼ in.	Stainless steel or galvanized

*See project resources on p. 179.

your tower will cascade with a lush dis-play of fruits and flowers.

When we sat down to design the Strawberry Tower, we originally intend-ed to use a separate finial at the top. But during one of our frequent trips to the lumberyard, we noticed a gothic-style cedar fence post that promised to sim-plify the construction of our project as well as lower its cost.

The tower is constructed by attaching four L-shaped frame sections to a center post with hardwood dowels. Since the frame sections extend directly out from the four corners, we had to create flat surfaces to accept the ends of the frames. With the frame constructed, it's just a matter of adding a series of pro-gressively smaller soil-retaining boards to hold in the dirt. Once you set up

Once your Strawberry Tower is complete, place it on a level spot in your garden.

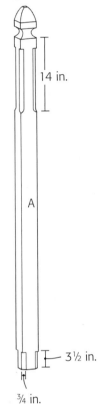

14 in.

A

3½ in.

¾ in.

Strawberry Tower frame board profile

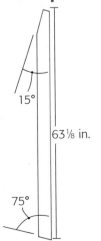

15°

63⅛ in.

75°

the flat surface joints. These would total four small cuts 3½ in. from the bottom of the post and four cuts 2 in. below the base of the finial. Set the adjustable base of your sabersaw to 45°, then starting at the bottom of the post, trim the four corners until you reach the cuts made with the backsaw. Follow the same procedure to create the flat surfaces below the finial, starting your cuts about 14 in. below the cuts made with the backsaw. The top illustration at right shows what these surfaces should look like when you're finished. Each flat surface should be about ¾ in. wide and ½ in. deep.

3 To construct the four L-shaped sections that attach to the center post, cut all of the side frame boards (C), as shown in the bottom illustration at right. Attach one bottom frame board (B) to each side frame board with a pair of dowels, as shown in the illustration at left on p. 116. Use a doweling jig to accurately place the holes for each dowel pin. When all four frame sections are complete, attach them to the center post. Use a doweling jig to drill two holes in each end of the frame sections, then use four dowel centers to locate the position of the holes on the center post (dowel centers slip into the holes in the frame and have a point on the opposite end, which leaves a mark on the post when the frame is pushed into place). Drill the matching holes in the center post and install the four frame sections using four dowel pins for each frame. Allow the joints to dry at least 24 hours.

4 Next, install the four bottom trim boards (D), as shown in the illustration at right on p. 116. Notice that the ends of these boards have a 45° bevel (see the top illustration on p. 117). Attach these boards at the bottom of the tower frame

your table saw to make the compound cuts necessary on the retaining boards, trimming and installing the boards goes rather quickly. The retaining boards also lock the entire frame together, making a sturdy structure that should last for years.

1 Trim all of the boards to size. It's a good idea to trim the soil–retaining boards (E thru N) about ⅛ in. to ¼ in. full so they can be custom–fitted to the frame during assembly. Trim the overall length of the center post (A) to 6 ft.

2 Begin by creating the flat surfaces along the edges of the post where the four frames attach (see the top illustration at right). Use a backsaw to make ½–in.–deep cuts at one end of each of

Strawberry Tower frame assembly

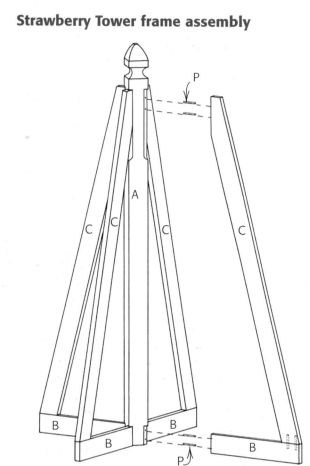

Strawberry Tower soil-retaining board assembly

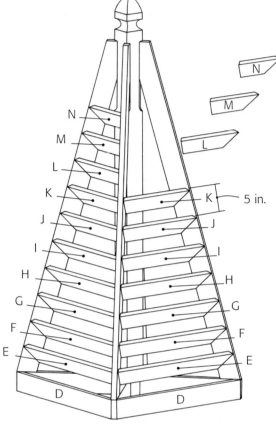

with two wood screws (R) at either end. Drive each screw through the bottom trim board, then into the bottom frame board. Always predrill each screw hole to prevent the wood from splitting, especially when they are being installed near an edge.

5 Prepare the 10 soil-retaining boards (E thru N) for installation by making compound cuts. Once your table saw is set up for the first compound cut, the rest will go faster than you might expect. First, set the miter gauge to 60°,

then tilt the sawblade to 35°. These set-tings will produce the chamfer along each of the miter cuts. To produce both compound cuts on each soil-retaining board, position the miter gauge to the left of the sawblade, but reposition it to the opposite 60° mark for the second cut. Try cutting a couple of test pieces until you're comfortable with making the two cuts. Because the frame may not be perfectly symmetrical, it's best to cut each of the retainer boards a bit full. If necessary, you can trim the boards after testing them in the frame.

Strawberry Tower soil-retaining board profiles

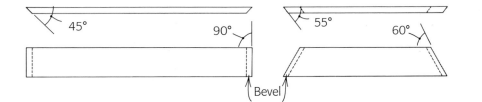

PROFILES OF BOTTOM TRIM BOARD

45° 90°

Bevel

PROFILES OF SOIL-RETAINING BOARD

55° 60°

6 Install each set of retainer boards 5 in. above the previous set (as measured along the edge of the side frame board). We found it helpful to pencil the position of each set of retainer boards, including the 35° angle they form in the frame. Use two wood screws (R) to attach each end of the soil-retainer boards.

7 After the retainer boards are in, install the top trim boards (O) (see the illustration at right). These boards are cut with simple 45° miters and give the frame a finished look. Secure each one with two 4d galvanized finishing nails (Q). Drive these nails through the trim boards near each mitered edge, then into the top of the side frame boards. For added stability, we also hammered in four nails near the edge of each miter joint to lock them together.

8 Finish the tower, if desired. If you make the tower out of a rot-resistant wood such as cedar or redwood, it's not necessary to add a preservative or finish to the final structure. However, we wanted to extend the life of our tower, so we applied an oil-based semitransparent stain. If you do apply a stain or preservative, read the label carefully to make sure it is nontoxic when cured. Let

the tower sit out in the weather for at least two or three weeks.

9 After placing the new Strawberry Tower in the garden or other chosen site, fill it with soil. Remove one of the soil-retaining boards about halfway up the tower so you can fill up the bulk of the space using a shovel (see the photo at right). Fill the upper half of the tower using a small scoop or trowel. After watering the soil thoroughly, you can begin planting your strawberries. Throughout the summer, check the soil's moisture daily. The soil in the upper tiers will dry out more quickly than the soil in the tiers at the base of the tower.

Temporarily remove one of the retaining boards to fill the tower with soil. Water and lightly compact the soil as you go.

Strawberry Tower trim board assembly

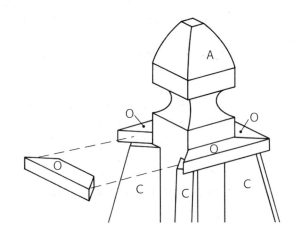

GREENHOUSE

A greenhouse can be enjoyed on many levels. Not only does it provide an environment for growing and propagating plants but it can also be a place to relax after a busy day. In addition, a classically designed greenhouse can be an architectural focal point in your landscape.

This 12-ft. by 18-ft. glass greenhouse offers all of the above. The split-face concrete block foundation gives the structure its classic look. Equally traditional is the paving stone floor that provides a level surface for the placement of a small table and chair set. During the busy spring months, the furniture can be replaced with an additional propagation bench. Further enhancing this structure's classic architectural lines is its steep-pitched roof. It provides plenty of overhead area for hanging plants and aids in shedding snow. Without a doubt, this greenhouse will become a beautiful addition to your landscape and, if you're like us, a favorite year-round retreat.

A greenhouse offers warmth to plants and a haven for gardeners while adding architectural interest to the landscape.

GREENHOUSE MATERIALS LIST

Key	Qty.	Description	Finished Dimensions	Material
Frame				
A	2	Sill plates	1½ in. x 7½ in. x 56 in.	Treated lumber
B	1	Sill plate	1½ in. x 7½ in. x 144 in.	Treated lumber
C	2	Sill plates	1½ in. x 7½ in. x 216 in.	Treated lumber
D	2	Eave plates	1½ in. x 5½ in. x 214 in.	Cedar
E	2	Bottom plates	1½ in. x 3½ in. x 214 in.	Cedar
F	1	Bottom plate	1½ in. x 3½ in. x 135 in.	Cedar
G	2	Bottom plates	1½ in. x 3½ in. x 51½ in.	Cedar
H	20	Side wall studs	1½ in. x 3½ in. x 36¾ in.	Cedar
I	4	End wall studs	1½ in. x 3½ in. x 40½ in.	Cedar
J	4	End wall studs	1½ in. x 3½ in. x 60 in.	Cedar
K	4	End wall studs	1½ in. x 3½ in. x 79½ in.	Cedar
L	1	End wall stud	1½ in. x 3½ in. x 45½ in.	Cedar
M	1	End wall stud	1½ in. x 3½ in. x 88¾ in.	Cedar
N	1	Roof ridge	1½ in. x 5½ in. x 214 in.	Cedar
O	1	Ridge extension	1½ in. x 3½ in. x 214 in.	Cedar
P	1	Ridge cap	¾ in. x 5½ in. x 214 in.	Cedar
Q	20	Rafters	1½ in. x 3½ in. x 89½ in.	Cedar
R	1	Door eave	1½ in. x 5½ in. x 32 in.	Cedar
S	4	Ridge blocks	1½ in. x 3½ in. x 17¼ in.	Cedar
T	14	Ridge blocks	1½ in. x 3½ in. x 23½ in.	Cedar
U	8	Vent blocks	1½ in. x 3½ in. x 23½ in.	Cedar
V	4	Eave blocks	1½ in. x 3½ in. x 17¼ in.	Cedar
W	14	Eave blocks	1½ in. x 3½ in. x 23½ in.	Cedar
X	28	Side glass rails	¾ in. x 1½ in. x 35¼ in.	Cedar
Y	4	End glass rails	¾ in. x 1½ in. x 38½ in.	Cedar
Z	4	End glass rails	¾ in. x 1½ in. x 56¼ in.	Cedar

GREENHOUSE MATERIALS LIST continued

BA	4	End glass rails	¾ in. x 1½ in. x 58 in.	Cedar
BB	4	End glass rails	¾ in. x 1½ in. x 75¾ in.	Cedar
BC	2	End glass rails	¾ in. x 1½ in. x 77½ in.	Cedar
BD	2	End glass rails	¾ in. x 1½ in. x 34½ in.	Cedar
BE	2	End glass rails	¾ in. x 1½ in. x 45½ in.	Cedar
BF	2	End glass rails	¾ in. x 1½ in. x 88¾ in.	Cedar
BG	20	Roof glass rails	¾ in. x 1½ in. x 87½ in.	Cedar
BH	16	Roof glass rails	¾ in. x 1½ in. x 69 in.	Cedar
BI	8	Window stops	¾ in. x 1½ in. x 23½ in.	Cedar
BJ	8	Window stops	¾ in. x 1½ in. x 33¾ in.	Cedar
BK	8	Roof braces	1½ in. x 3½ in. x 47 in.	Cedar
BL	32	Gussets	¾ in. x 3½ in. x 10 in.	Cedar
BM	1	Roof rail	1½ in. x 3½ in. x 207 in.	Cedar
BN	2	Roof rail brace	1½ in. x 3½ in. x 41½ in.	Cedar
BO	4	Gussets	¾ in. x 3½ in. x 8 in.	Cedar
BP	4	Gussets	¾ in. x 3½ in. x 8 in.	Cedar
BQ	4	Gussets	¾ in. x 3½ in. x 16 in.	Cedar

Vents and Windows

BR	4	Vent frame boards	¾ in. x 2½ in. x 53 in.	Cedar
BS	12	Vent frame boards	¾ in. x 2 in. x 17¼ in.	Cedar
BT	4	Vent frame boards	¾ in. x 2 in. x 53 in.	Cedar
BU	4	Vent cap boards	¾ in. x 3⅛ in. x 53 in.	Cedar
BV	12	Vent cap boards	¾ in. x 2 in. x 19¼ in.	Cedar
BW	8	Vent glass	¹⁄₁₆ in. x 18 in. x 24 in.	Window glass
BX	8	Plugs	³⁄₁₆ in. x ⅜ in. x ¾ in.	Cedar
BY	8	Window frame boards	1 in. x 2 in. x 23¼ in.	Cedar
BZ	8	Window frame boards	1 in. x 2 in. x 35 in.	Cedar
CA	4	Window glass	¹⁄₁₆ in. x 20 in. x 31¾ in.	Window glass

continued

GREENHOUSE MATERIALS LIST continued

CB	8	Window molding	⅜ in. x ½ in. x 20¼ in.	Cedar
CC	8	Window molding	⅜ in. x ½ in. x 32 in.	Cedar

Glass and Caps

CD	4	Side wall glass	1/16 in. x 17¾ in. x 36 in.	Window glass
CE	10	Side wall glass	1/16 in. x 24 in. x 36 in.	Window glass
CF	8	End wall glass	1/16 in. x 24 in. x 36 in.	Window glass
CG	8	End wall glass	1/16 in. x 24 in. x 21¾ in.	Window glass
CH	4	End wall glass	1/16 in. x 24 in. x 20¼ in.	Window glass
CI	2	End wall glass	1/16 in. x 15¾ in. x 24 in.	Window glass
CJ	2	End wall glass	1/16 in. x 15¾ in. x 22¾ in.	Window glass
CK	2	End wall glass	1/16 in. x 15¾ in. x 36 in.	Window glass
CL	2	End wall glass	1/16 in. x 15¾ in. x 36 in.	Window glass
CM	2	End wall glass	1/16 in. x 15¾ in. x 19 in.	Window glass
CN	8	Roof glass	1/16 in. x 17¾ in. x 30 in.	Window glass
CO	4	Roof glass	1/16 in. x 17¾ in. x 29¼ in.	Window glass
CP	28	Roof glass	1/16 in. x 24 in. x 30 in.	Window glass
CQ	6	Roof glass	1/16 in. x 24 in. x 29¼ in.	Window glass
CR	8	Roof glass	1/16 in. x 24 in. x 10¾ in.	Window glass
CS	4	Side wall caps	¾ in. x 1½ in. x 107 in.	Cedar
CT	12	Side wall caps	¾ in. x 2¼ in. x 35¾ in	Cedar
CU	8	Side wall caps	¾ in. x 3 in. x 35¾ in.	Cedar
CV	4	End wall caps	¾ in. x 2¼ in. x 39 in.	Cedar
CW	4	End wall caps	¾ in. x 3 in. x 58⅜ in.	Cedar
CX	4	End wall caps	¾ in. x 3 in. x 77⅞ in.	Cedar
CY	1	End wall cap	¾ in. x 3 in. x 45½ in.	Cedar
CZ	1	End wall cap	¾ in. x 3 in. x 89¼ in.	Cedar
DA	4	End wall caps	¾ in. x 1½ in. x 90¾ in.	Cedar
DB	4	Roof caps	¾ in. x 2¼ in. x 91 in.	Cedar

GREENHOUSE MATERIALS LIST continued

DC	16	Roof caps	¾ in. x 3 in. x 91 in.	Cedar
DD	4	Roof caps	¾ in. x 2¾ in. x 15¾ in.	Cedar
DE	14	Roof caps	¾ in. x 2¾ in. x 22 in.	Cedar
DF	8	Roof caps	¾ in. x 1½ in. x 22 in.	Cedar
Door and Finials				
DG	2	Door frame boards	1 in. x 3½ in. x 80½ in.	Cedar
DH	1	Door frame board	1 in. x 3½ in. x 32 in.	Cedar
DI	2	Door stop boards	¾ in. x 1½ in. x 79¾ in.	Cedar
DJ	1	Door stop board	¾ in. x 1½ in. x 30 in.	Cedar
DK	1	Door	1⅜ in. x 30 in. x 80 in.	Commercially made
DL	2	Finials	2 in. x 2 in. x 23¾ in.	Cedar
Hardware				
DM*	5 lbs.	Wood screws	#8 x 2½ in.	Stainless steel
DN*	5 lbs.	Wood screws	#8 x 2 in.	Stainless steel
DO*	2 lbs.	Wood screws	#7 x 1½ in.	Stainless steel
DP*	40	Wood screws	#6 x 1¼ in.	Stainless steel
DQ*	16	Hinges	2 in. x 2 in.	Stainless steel or brass
DR	190	Escutcheon pins	18 x ¾ in.	Brass
DS*	108	Lap clips	⅜ in. x ½ in.	Stainless steel
DT*	48	Dowel pins	¼ in. x 2 in.	Hardwood
DU*	12	Glazing tape	⅛ in. x ⅜ in. x 75 ft.	Closed-cell foam
DV*	2	Hinges	3½ in.	Stainless steel or brass
DW	1	Door lockset	Standard	Brass or nickel plated
DX*	4	Vent openers	18-in. max. opening	Aluminum
DY	4	Turn buttons	1¾ in.	Zinc plated
DZ*	4	Concrete screws	3/16 in. x 2¾ in.	Steel
EA*	6	Wood plugs	⅜ in. x ½ in.	Hardwood

*See project resources on p. 179.   Quantities listed for screws and nails are approximations.

BEFORE YOU BEGIN

Before you begin constructing your greenhouse, there are a few important things to keep in mind.

You should choose the location for your greenhouse carefully. Don't locate a glass greenhouse under or near any large trees. Branches dislodged in a storm can easily break the glass. If possible, align the ridge of the greenhouse in an east–west direction to best take advantage of the sun in early spring. A location that benefits from a natural windbreak is also a plus. Finally, make sure it isn't too far from utilities if you plan to bring in electricity and water.

We decided on glass for the covering because of its traditional look and appeal, but you could also use a rigid plastic glazing. A plastic cover is more durable but is much more expensive to install and may scratch or dull over time. We designed this greenhouse to make use of standard–size pieces of glass. Unfortunately, there is still a fair amount that will need to be cut. Cutting glass is not that difficult (see the sidebar on glass cutting on pp. 140–141), but if you feel uncomfortable about it, you can buy the standard–size pieces in bulk and have a glass shop cut the rest for you.

All of the screws used to construct this greenhouse are stainless steel. These screws are strong and have better corrosion resistance than galvanized screws. Another problem with galvanized screws is that they tend to leave black stains when used in cedar and redwood. The rest of the hardware was selected for its resistance to corrosion as well, including stainless steel and brass hinges.

In the materials list, we suggest using full 18-ft. lengths for some of the framing lumber: roof ridge, bottom plates, sill plates, and eave plates. While these lengths may need to be special ordered, it is preferable to use them to avoid splicing shorter lengths together.

Be aware, as with all construction, that there may be small measurement differences between what is listed on the plans and what you may actually find to be the case. This can happen for a number of reasons, such as dimensional variations in your wood, warping, and cuts being slightly off. As always, it's a good policy to measure twice and cut once. Pay particular attention to the top pieces of glass in the roof runs and in the end walls. You will want to take an exact measurement for these pieces or actually hold the pieces of glass in place and use a pen to mark the precise score lines.

Finally, take your time, be safety conscious, and make the construction process an enjoyable one.

FOUNDATION AND UTILITIES

While it is not within the scope of this book to completely discuss the construction of the foundation or installation of utilities, a few thoughts about how we approached these aspects are in order.

The process of building the foundation wall may seem a bit daunting to some, but like all things, it's amazing what you can do when you put your mind to it. This was our first block wall and even though it took us a painfully long time (by professional standards) to construct, we remained patient and it turned out quite nicely. We chose a split–faced cinder block that has the appearance of stone, as opposed to the commercial look of regular smooth block. It took 203 full-size cinder blocks and four half-size blocks to create the wall (see the illustration below for the exact measurements of the footing and wall). We designed the greenhouse to use standard block sizes; no cutting is necessary. If you prefer, you could substitute brick or stone for the cinder block, as long as you keep the dimensions the same.

There are many excellent books devoted entirely to building foundations and walls. However, if you don't feel comfortable with this part of the project, you may want to hire a contractor. You can still save a great deal of money on the project by doing the rest of the work yourself.

You may also want professional help when installing the utilities. Depending on the types of plants you want to grow, electricity, water, and heat may be necessary components of your new green-

A cement footing and foundation wall are the first elements of the Greenhouse to be installed. If you're short on time or inexperienced with cement work, consider hiring a contractor for this portion of the construction.

Greenhouse foundation wall

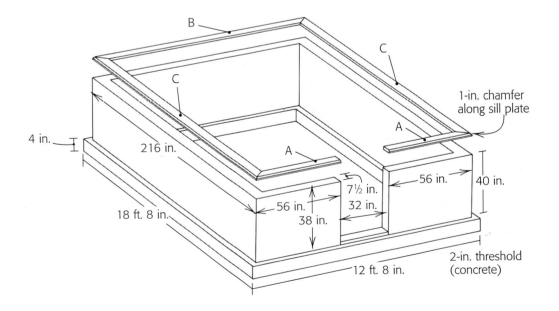

4 in.

216 in.

1-in. chamfer along sill plate

A

A

56 in.

40 in.

7½ in.

32 in.

56 in.

38 in.

18 ft. 8 in.

B

C

C

A

2-in. threshold (concrete)

12 ft. 8 in.

The flooring is the interior's finishing touch.

GREENHOUSE FRAME

1 Once the foundation wall is completed, cement in place a set of anchor bolts that will be used to secure the sill plates (A, B, C) to the top of the wall. We used eight anchor bolts along each side wall and six along each end wall. Position all of the anchor bolts about 2¾ in. from the outside edge of the wall, with the ends of the bolts extending about 2 in. above the top of the wall. This positioning will hide the ends of the bolts underneath the bottom plates of the stud walls.

Mark the positions of the bolts on the undersides of the sill plates and drill a slightly larger hole at each mark. The sill plates have a 1-in. chamfer cut along the outside edge (see the illustration on p. 125). The corners are cut at 45° angles, while the ends at the door opening are cut off square. Install the sill plates and secure them with the nuts and washers that match the anchor bolts.

2 Install the side walls first. Each side wall consists of the top eave plate (D), bottom plate (E), and 10 side wall studs (H). The eave plate has a chamfered edge that overhangs the wall to the outside, as shown in the illustrations on the facing page. Assemble the side wall as an entire unit if possible, or make it in two pieces and set in place along the top edge of the sill plate chamfer as shown. Use two wood screws (DM) at each junction of a wall stud and eave plate or bottom plate. Notice that the two end openings in this wall measure 17¼ in., while the middle openings measure 23½ in. Attach each wall section to the sill plates with two wood screws (DM) between each end wall stud.

house. Plan for these utilities before you start construction, as it is easier to run all the lines into the greenhouse before the foundation is built.

Two more additions worth mentioning are the French drains and the greenhouse floor. Instead of gutters, we dug 1-ft.-wide and 1-ft.-deep troughs along the footing of the greenhouse directly under the eaves. We edged these troughs with 2x6s and filled them with pea gravel. These French drains collect excess rainwater and minimize the amount of dirt splashed on the cinder block walls.

The greenhouse floor can be finished in a number of ways. We decided on a middle platform of distressed paver blocks, framed on three sides by pea gravel. This type of floor will easily absorb the amount of water typically used inside a greenhouse. Other options include the use of brick, gravel, concrete, or even a treated-wood floor.

Elevation view of Greenhouse frame

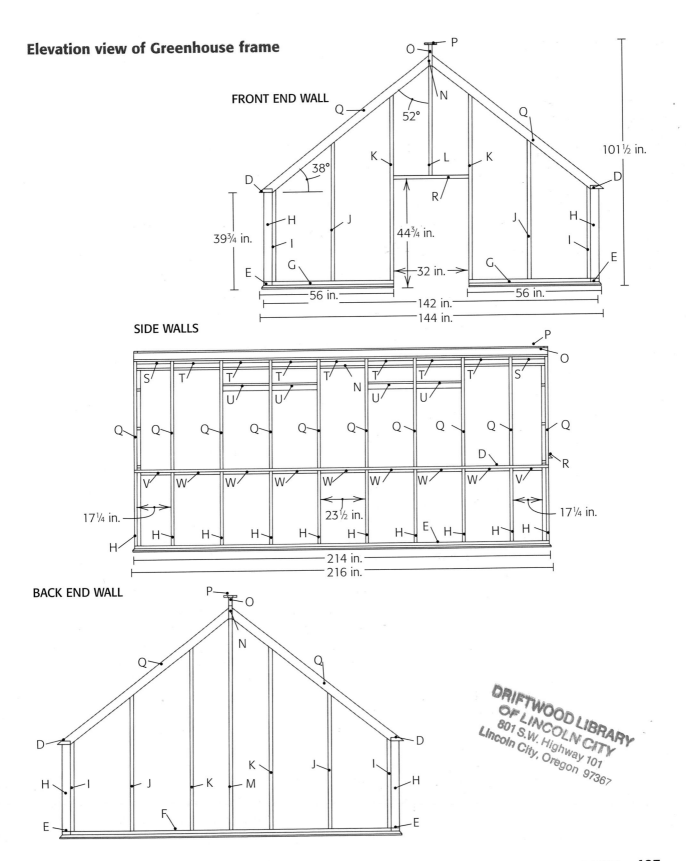

FRONT END WALL

O P
N
52°
Q
K L K
R
38°
D D
H J J H
I I
39¾ in.
44¾ in.
E G G E
32 in.
56 in. 56 in.
142 in.
144 in.
101½ in.

SIDE WALLS

P
O
S T T T T T T T S
N
U U U U
Q Q Q Q Q Q Q Q Q Q
D
R
V W W W W W W W V
17¼ in.
23½ in.
17¼ in.
H H H H H H H E H H H
H
214 in.
216 in.

BACK END WALL

P O
N
Q Q
D D
K J
H I J K M I H
F
E E

Greenhouse door eave board

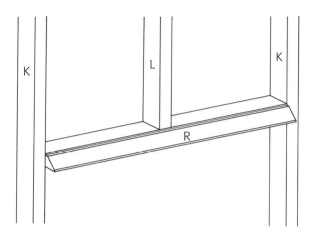

3 Next, temporarily support the roof ridge (N) until the rafters (Q) can be screwed in place. We built two supports in the shape of an inverted "T" out of 2x4s and screwed them on top of the sill plates at each end of the greenhouse. We also attached angle braces to each vertical 2x4 in the "T" to prevent it from swaying. We then set the roof ridge in place with the bottom edge of the roof ridge 90¼ in. above the top of the sill plate. We also nailed small pieces of 1x2s to the roof ridge and 2x4 support to prevent the ridge from falling. The ends of the roof ridge should be in the same plane as the ends of the side walls. You will also need to temporarily prop up the middle of the ridge with a similar type of support.

4 Cut all of the rafters (Q) to length, creating the bird's-mouth cut at one end and the proper angle cut at the other (see the illustration on the facing page). Install the rafter boards as shown in the illustrations on p. 127 with wood screws

(DM). Each rafter board should line up with a side wall stud below it. Notice that the top end of each rafter joins the ridge about 1 in. below the ridge's top edge.

5 With the rafters in place, remove the temporary supports for the roof ridge. To ensure that the frame stays in place when you remove these supports, nail two or three 12-ft. temporary crossties between both side walls just under the eave plate. This will keep the walls from leaning outward when the ridge supports are removed. For now, the center ridge support can remain in place.

6 Begin installing the two end walls by first screwing the bottom plates (F, G) in place along the top edge of the sill plate chamfer. Install all of the end wall studs (I through M), as detailed in the illustrations on p. 127. The tops of most of the end wall studs have a special cut to allow the outside edge of the stud to be flush with the outside face of the end rafters (see the bottom illustration on p. 130). The profile of this cut is shown in the illustration on the facing page. The tops of the end wall studs should sit at least 1½ in. below the edge of the rafter boards to allow room for the glass rails later on.

Both end walls are constructed in the same way, except for the area of the greenhouse door. Install the door eave (R) with wood screws (DM), as shown in the illustration above. The door eave has the same profile as the eave plates except for an added rabbet to prevent water from seeping in where the glass meets the door eave (see the illustration on the facing page). Secure the bottoms of each end wall stud with wood screws

Greenhouse board profile chart

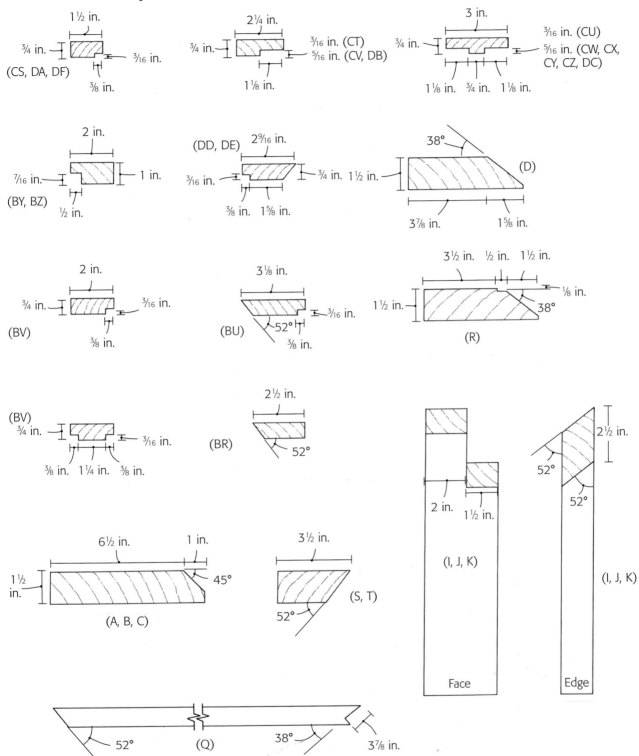

1½ in.

¾ in. ‖ 3/16 in.

(CS, DA, DF)

⅜ in.

2¼ in.

¾ in.   3/16 in. (CT)
        5/16 in. (CV, DB)

1⅛ in.

3 in.

¾ in.   3/16 in. (CU)
        5/16 in. (CW, CX, CY, CZ, DC)

1⅛ in.   ¾ in.   1⅛ in.

2 in.

7/16 in. ‖ 1 in.

(BY, BZ)

½ in.

(DD, DE) 2 9/16 in.

3/16 in.   ¾ in.   1½ in.

⅜ in.   1⅝ in.

38°

(D)

3⅞ in.   1⅝ in.

2 in.

¾ in.   3/16 in.

(BV)

⅜ in.

3⅛ in.

52°   3/16 in.

(BU)   ⅜ in.

3½ in.   ½ in.   1½ in.

1½ in.   ⅛ in.   38°

(R)

(BV)
¾ in.   3/16 in.

⅜ in.   1¼ in.   ⅜ in.

2½ in.

(BR)   52°

2 in.   1½ in.

(I, J, K)

Face

2½ in.

52°

52°

(I, J, K)

Edge

6½ in.   1 in.

1½ in.   45°

(A, B, C)

3½ in.

52°   (S, T)

52°   (Q)   38°   3⅞ in.

Greenhouse roof brace and gusset assembly

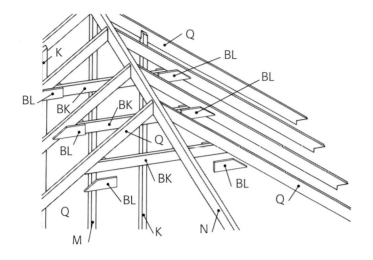

7 Next, attach the ridge extension (O) and the ridge cap (P). Before lifting the ridge extension in place, drill several ³⁄₈-in. holes along the top edge about every 2 ft. Make these holes 2 in. to 2½ in. deep. Using an extended bit on an electric screwdriver, drive in several wood screws (DM) through the bottoms of these pilot holes into the roof ridge (N) below. After the ridge extension is secure, attach the ridge cap to the top of the extension with wood screws (DN), as shown in the illustration below. The ends of the ridge cap are angle cut to match the 2-in. width of the finials (see the photo on p. 138).

(DM) driven at an angle (as you would toenail a standard wall stud). The tops are fastened to the rafters with the same screws.

Greenhouse frame in perspective

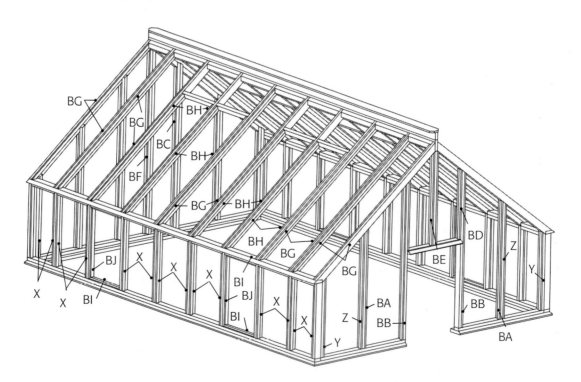

8 Install the ridge blocks (S, T), vent blocks (U), and eave blocks (V, W), as shown in the illustrations at right and on p. 127. The ridge blocks are beveled to match the roof pitch at the top end (see the profile in the illustration on p. 129). The other blocks are simply 2x4s cut to length. Attach all of the blocks with wood screws (DM).

9 Cut the glass rails (X through BH), which go on next, from common cedar 1x2s. The rails sit flush with the outside edges of the rafters, end wall studs, and side wall studs. Their purpose is to provide extra surface support for the glass. The only openings that don't have glass rails are the vents, windows, and front door. All of the rails that fasten to the end wall studs and rafters are cut to match the angles of the roof.

It's a good idea to measure each opening so that every rail fits snugly. Also, if the bottom end of a rafter board falls a bit short of the eave plate chamfer, you can position the end of the roof glass rails so that the glass makes a smooth transition from the rafter to the eave (see the middle illustration at right). Secure the glass rails with wood screws (DO) about every 2 ft.

10 Cut the window stops (BI, BJ) from cedar 1x2s. They provide a positive stop for each of the four hinged windows attached to the side walls. Set the window stops back 1 in. from the outside edge of the side wall studs with wood screws (DO), as shown in the bottom illustration at right.

Greenhouse installation of eave and vent blocks

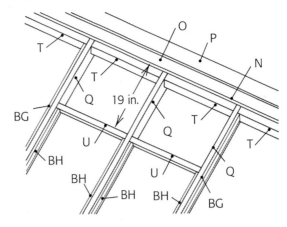

Greenhouse eave, glass rail, rafter, and wall stud junction

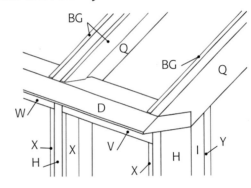

Greenhouse window attachment

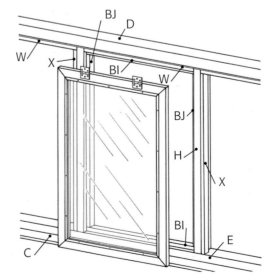

Greenhouse roof rail brace

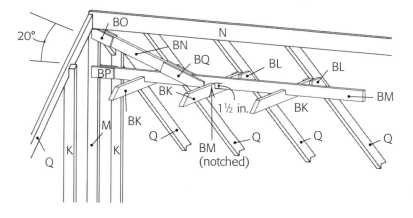

11 Cut the eight roof braces (BK) that will help prevent the frame from swaying side to side (see the illustration above). After cutting the first roof brace, use it as a template to cut the rest. Attach each roof brace to the rafters with one wood screw (DM) at each end, then cut the 32 gussets (BL). The beveled end of the gussets should fit snugly against the back edge of the roof glass rails. Secure each of the gussets with five wood screws (DO), three into the rafter and two into the roof brace.

12 Finally, install the roof rail (BM), as shown in the illustration above. This brace helps prevent the greenhouse from swaying end to end. It also doubles as a nice platform to carry light fixtures, an overhead hose, or hanging plants. The roof rail is notched to slip down over the middle of each roof brace 1½ in. Adding the roof rail braces (BN) gives even more protection to the frame. The three connection points at each end of the greenhouse are secured with three different gussets (BO, BP, BQ) as shown. Attach the gussets with wood screws (DO).

13 Now that the basic frame is completed, apply the preservative or finish of your choice. We used an oil–based, semitransparent stain that matched some of the other projects in our yard. Be especially generous in those areas that will receive the most exposure to rain, such as the eave plates.

GREENHOUSE VENTS AND WINDOWS

1 Begin by constructing the four greenhouse vent windows according to the instructions for the cold frame windows (see pp. 109–111). Assemble the vent frame boards (BR, BS, BT), as shown in the top illustration on the facing page, with dowel pins (DT). The glass (BW) sits against two brass escutcheon pins (DR) and is held securely in place by the vent cap boards (BU, BV). Apply glazing tape (DU) to the glass before screwing the vent caps in place with wood screws (DP). Two small plugs (BX) seal the rabbet exposed at each end of the vent. The profiles of the beveled top vent boards (BR, BU) are detailed in the illustration on p. 129.

2 Finish the vent windows to match the rest of the greenhouse frame, then install two hinges (DQ) about 6 in. from both ends of each vent, as shown in the bottom illustration on the facing page.

3 Before installing the roof vents, temporarily tack in place two ¾–in. cedar boards to simulate the width of the roof caps (see the bottom illustration on the facing page).

Greenhouse vent and window frame assembly

SIDE WINDOW

TOP WINDOW VENT

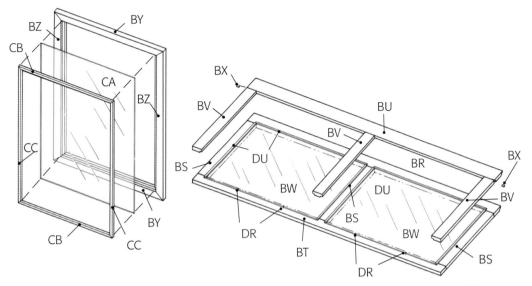

4 Next, set each roof vent in place and secure the hinges to the ridge extension with the screws provided in the package. Make sure the middle of the vent sits directly over the middle of the vent frame as shown in the illustration at right. Repeat this process for all four vent assemblies. The vents open and close using four automatic vent openers (DX), which are available from most greenhouse supply companies. Wait until the rest of the building is complete before you install the openers so they don't get in the way.

5 Construct the side window in a manner similar to that of a picture frame (see the illustration above). Cut the four window frame boards (BY, BZ) for each window from a cedar board with a rabbet along one edge (see the profile in the illustration on p. 129). Glue the 45° miters and join them with dowel pins (see the sidebar on dowel joints on p. 63).

Greenhouse vent window attachment

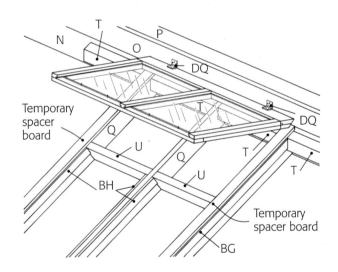

Temporary spacer board

Temporary spacer board

6 Once the glue is dry, apply the finish. Then add the window glass (CA), as shown in the top illustration on p. 133.

7 Cut the window molding (CB, CC) to size and miter the corners in a miter box. Finish each piece to match the rest of the greenhouse, then install the window molding with three or four brass escutcheon pins per side. The top of the molding should be flush with the face of the window frame.

8 Next, attach two hinges (DQ) at the top of each frame, as shown in the bottom illustration on p. 131. Set each window in place and center it in the opening against the window stops. Secure both hinges to the eave block. Before continuing, check to make sure each window swings freely.

9 Finish the side window installation by adding four turn buttons (DY) to the bottom plate below the window. The turn buttons hold the windows closed.

To prop the windows open, simply use a block of wood or use automatic vent openers as we did on the roof vents.

GREENHOUSE GLASS AND CAPS

No matter what area of the greenhouse you are covering in glass (side walls, end walls, or roof), the procedure is basically the same. Therefore, we will outline the procedure as opposed to talking about the individual pieces of glass. One important thing to keep in mind is that the glass panes are designed to overlap both the wall studs and the roof rafters by no more than $1/4$ in., since any more than that may interfere with the proper seating of the cap boards. Use the illustrations below and on the facing page along with the materials list to determine which piece of glass goes in a particular spot on the frame. Refer to the profile chart on p. 129 and the materials list to determine how to cut each of the

Greenhouse glass and cap boards—front wall

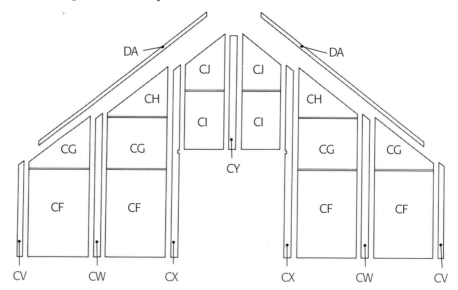

Greenhouse glass and cap boards—side walls and roof

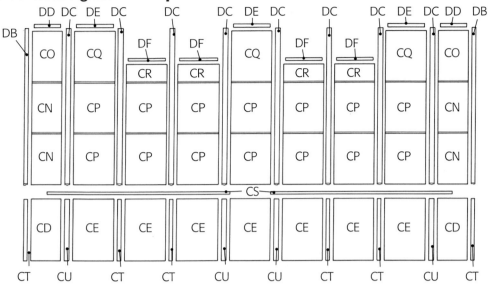

Greenhouse glass and cap boards—back wall

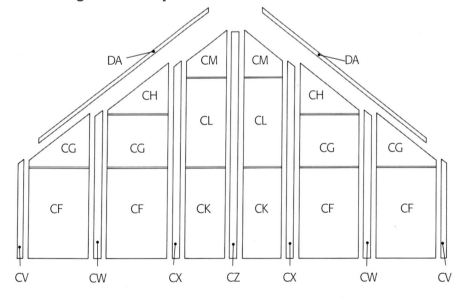

cap boards used to secure the glass. The cap boards are shown in their correct positions in the illustrations on the facing page and above as well. The photos on p. 136 also show the placement of most of the glass and cap pieces. Before installing the cap pieces, finish them to match the rest of the greenhouse.

Side Wall Glass Installation

1 Make a pencil line the width of each opening ½ in. below the top of the bottom plate. Tap in three or four evenly spaced brass escutcheon pins along this line. Set in place a sheet of side wall glass so that its bottom edge rests

Use duct tape to secure the glass to the wall studs until the cap boards are screwed in place.

As you install the roof glass, it will be necessary to work from inside and outside the Greenhouse. Use two ladders, placing one at each location.

against the escutcheon pins. Have two pieces of duct tape ready to tape the glass to the side wall studs on either side. Repeat this step until all of the glass (CD, CE) is in place along one side.

2 Apply a single layer of glazing tape (DU) along the top and both sides of each piece of glass. The tape should be applied along the edge of the frame opening, not along the edge of the glass. By doing this, when you install the cap board, the inside edge of the glazing tape will match the edge of the cap board.

3 Before setting the top side wall caps (CS) in place, mark the position of the four window hinges and cut a small ⅛-in. recess in the back of the boards to allow clearance for the hinges. Then set the caps in place and secure them with wood screws (DN).

4 Next, install the rest of the side wall caps (CT, CU), also securing them with wood screws (DN). Repeat this process for the other side.

End Wall Glass Installation

1 Tap in four escutcheon pins along the pencil line as you did for the side walls. Set the first piece of glass in place and tape it to the end wall studs with duct tape. Place two lap clips (DS) along the top edge of the glass (lap clips are flat, S-shaped clips available through greenhouse supply companies). Lap clips allow each successive piece of glass to overlap the previous one by a consistent ½ in., thereby creating a shingled effect.

2 After carefully measuring and cutting the next piece of glass, set the bottom edge in the lap clips and tape this piece to the end wall studs. Install the rest of the end wall glass as detailed in the illustrations on pp. 134–135.

3 When you've completed installing the glass for one of the end walls, run a double layer of glazing tape around three sides of each vertical run. There are deeper rabbets in the end wall cap boards than there were for the side walls. The deeper rabbet is to accommodate the overlapping panes of glass. Since the glazing tape is only 1/8 in. thick, two layers are necessary. Leave an area 2 in. to 3 in. above each overlap with only one thickness of glazing tape. This will avoid too much pressure on the overlapped glass when the caps are tightened down. The completed end wall, minus the cap boards, should look as shown in the top photo on the facing page.

4 Install end wall cap boards (DA) first. Each of these cap boards should end 1 in. from the center of the ridge board to leave room for the finial (DL). Next, install the rest of the end wall caps (CV through CZ) with wood screws (DN). Repeat this process for the opposite end wall. Both use glass pieces (CF through CM).

Roof Glass Installation

Installing the roof glass (CN through CR) is easier than installing the end wall glass because you won't need to tape each piece of glass in place. Each run of glass, consisting of three panes, should stay in place until the cap boards are secured. However, and there's always a catch, you will need to work from one end of the greenhouse to the other—completing one run at a time. If you tried to put all of the glass on before installing the glazing tape or cap boards, you would soon find that there is no easy way to reach the middle runs. The bottom photo on the facing page shows the glass being installed one run at a time across the roof.

1 Other than the order for putting on the glass and cap boards, install the roof glass in the same manner as for the end walls. Temporarily prop up the vent windows while you install the glass and cap boards around each vent as shown in the bottom photo on the facing page.

2 Place the escutcheon pins 1/2 in. below the top edge of the eave chamfer.

3 For each roof run, set the glass in place using two lap clips between each sheet. Apply a double thickness of glazing tape before installing each appropriate roof cap (DB through DF). (Remember to use a single layer of glazing tape in the areas where the glass overlaps.) As with the rest of the cap boards, use wood screws (DN) spaced about every 2 ft.

GREENHOUSE DOOR AND FINIALS

Once all of the glass is in place, the urge to start filling the greenhouse with plants will be uncontrollable for most gardeners (Jan had ours half full at this point). But in order to make it completely usable, it will need a door.

Greenhouse door assembly

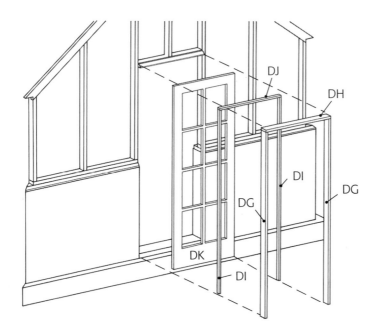

We designed the door opening to fit a standard 30-in. door. However, you will need to make your own door frame to finish the rough opening.

1 After cutting to size the door frame boards (DG, DH) and the door stop boards (DI, DJ), attach the door frame boards to the inside of the rough opening with wood screws (DM) and cement screws (DZ) (see the illustration at left). Once you drill pilot holes for the cement screws, you can drive the screws into the mortar between the cinder blocks without the need for plastic anchors.

2 Attach the door stop boards 1⅜ in. from the inside edge of the door frame.

3 Make any necessary adjustments to the door. We purchased a lightweight interior door (DK) to use for the greenhouse because the exterior doors are thicker and much heavier. However, we had to add silicone caulking around each windowpane and molding in the door to prevent water from ruining or warping the wood. We also had to trim the width of the door by about ¼ in.

4 Finish the door frame, door stops, and door with the same finish used on the rest of the greenhouse, then mount the door to the frame using two brass hinges (DV). With the addition of a standard lock set (DW), the greenhouse is almost complete.

5 Add the two finials (DL) at either end of the roof ridge to give a more finished look. The dimensions of the finials are detailed in the illustration on the facing page. To make the finials, follow the procedure we used for making the finial for the Pole Bean Trellis (see pp. 40–42).

The finials are the exterior's finishing touch.

6 Attach the finials to the roof ridge and ridge extension using three wood screws (DM) each. First drill a ⅜–in. pilot hole about 1 in. deep in the face of the finial and drive the screws from within this hole. Seal the hole with ⅜–in. wood plugs (EA), then apply the same finish to the finials as was used for the rest of the greenhouse.

Here are two final thoughts on the Greenhouse construction. First, apply silicone sealant to any seam where water may be a problem, including the top edge of the end wall cap (DA). Second, to cut down on drafts coming in under the door, install a door sweep along the bottom edge.

Completing a project like the Greenhouse will give you a great sense of accomplishment, as well as a wonderful place to hide when the world is moving just a little too fast.

Greenhouse finial profile

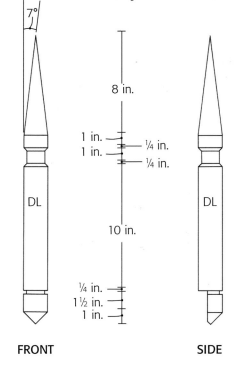

7°

8 in.

1 in.
1 in.
¼ in.
¼ in.

DL

10 in.

DL

¼ in.
1½ in.
1 in.

FRONT   SIDE

Once complete, the Greenhouse is a cozy retreat for plants and gardeners.

Cutting Glass

To score a piece of glass, apply a slight amount of downward pressure as you draw the glass cutter toward you.

Learning how to cut glass can have many practical applications, not the least of which is being able to resize broken panes to fit new projects. In this book, there are three projects that require custom panes of glass: the Cold Frame, the Greenhouse, and the Seed Saver's Box. If you rarely need a custom piece of glass, it may be practical to have a glass shop or hardware store cut it for you. But if you plan to build a structure like the Greenhouse, being able to cut your own glass can really save you money. Here's our method for cutting glass that has produced very few bad cuts.

The few tools you will need are readily available—a glass cutter, a straightedge or ruler, a fine-point permanent marker, a small can of household oil, a strip of no-slide foam, and a homemade snapping tool cut from a piece of 1x2 wood.

1. Use the ruler and permanent marker to draw a reference line on the glass where you will make your first score.

2. Place the foam strip about ½ in. to the left of your line as shown in the photo at left. Then set the ruler on the foam with the edge about ⅛ in. off your reference line. Position the glass cutter against the ruler and check to see that the cutting wheel is directly on your reference line. If not, adjust the position of the ruler until it is. Once the ruler is in position, you're ready to score the glass.

3. Put a drop of oil on the cutting wheel, then place the cutter on your reference line at the top of the glass. Apply a slight amount of downward pressure as you draw the glass cutter toward you. The cutter should leave an evenly scored line across the entire piece of glass. If not, try it again. Learning the right amount of pressure takes a little practice, but it's not difficult.

4. Once the glass is scored, snap off the unwanted piece. This is the part that usually makes people nervous. However, if the glass is properly scored it should snap cleanly along the line. We came up with a simple homemade tool that will make this step easier. Find a piece of scrap 1x2 wood about 3 ft. long. Run it through your table saw to cut a ¾-in.-deep groove along one edge of the board. Next, position the glass so that the scored line runs along the edge of the table with the piece to be snapped off hanging over the edge. Insert the unwanted piece of glass into the groove in the 1x2. Place your left hand on the glass and gently push down on the 1x2 with your right hand. The unwanted piece should snap cleanly along the line because this tool distributes the pressure evenly along the score.

It's always a good idea to practice on a few scrap pieces first. If the glass you're trying to cut doesn't break properly along the entire length of the scored line, you can often remedy the problem by using a pair of standard adjustable pliers to snap off any leftover remnants.

This simple homemade tool will make it easier to snap off the unwanted piece of glass.

Garden Tools and Accessories

The tool selection in any comprehensive garden catalog can bewilder even the most avid home gardener. But there are a few tools and garden accessories that have withstood the test of time to emerge as indispensable classics. This chapter highlights five such designs. They are tools and accessories that improve your soil, make your garden look neat, save you time, and organize your spring planting. Whether you make the Garden Sieve, Line and Reel Row Marker, Plant Caddy, Flat and Flat Dibble, or Seed Saver's Box, they will all provide years of service and bring a bit of nostalgia to your tool shed.

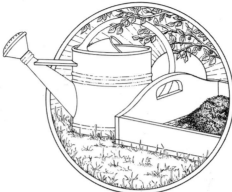

Compost is one of the best soil amendments available. Unfortunately, the variety of materials we compost decompose at different rates. A compost heap may look dark, crumbly, and ready to use, but concealed in the center may be partially decomposed vegetable matter such as the stubborn remnants of a corncob. A sieve is the perfect tool for sorting out these large chunks. Similarly, a sieve can be used to sort pebbles and debris from your garden.

The design of this sturdy Garden Sieve has been popular for decades. It features handle holes that are large enough for gloved hands or for a pair of hands if two people are shaking the sieve. Its 30-in. length allows it to be set on top of a garden cart or wheelbarrow while being filled. And the 1/4-in. mesh screen produces a finely filtered soil that's perfect for all your planting needs. This tool is easy to construct, simple to use, and a must for every gardener's tool shed.

This classic Garden Sieve is easy to construct and is indispensable in the garden.

GARDEN SIEVE MATERIALS LIST

Key	Qty.	Description	Finished Dimensions	Material
A	2	End boards	¾ in. x 7 in. x 24 in.	Pine, poplar, or fir
B	2	Side boards	¾ in. x 3½ in. x 28½ in.	Pine, poplar, or fir
C	2	Bottom boards	¾ in. x ¾ in. x 24 in.	Pine, poplar, or fir
D	2	Bottom boards	¾ in. x ¾ in. x 28½ in.	Pine, poplar, or fir
E	1	Wire screen	23½ in. x 29½ in.	¼-in. mesh screen
F	36	Wire screen staples	10 x ½ in.	Steel
G	20	Wood screws	#8 x 2 in.	Galvanized

Although generously sized, this sieve can be used by one person. The handles are large enough to accommodate two hands if two people are shaking the sieve.

The Garden Sieve can be made from a wide assortment of woods and still give years of service. We made ours out of poplar because it is strong, relatively inexpensive, and easy to cut. Unlike some wood frame sieves, we designed this one with bottom trim boards to prevent snagging your clothes or hands on the sharp ends of the wire screen. The trim also helps to hold the screen securely in place.

1 Cut the pieces given in the materials list and sand them smooth. Use the pattern grid at left on the facing page to lay out the two end boards (A). Once the pattern is transferred to the end boards, use a sabersaw to cut the top contour and the handle openings.

2 Attach the two side boards (B) to the end boards with two wood screws (G) at each corner (see the top illustration at right on the facing page).

3 With the basic frame assembled, turn the sieve over and lay the ¼-in. wire screen (E) on the bottom edge of the sieve. Position the screen so there is a ¼-in. space between the edge of the sieve and the screen on all four sides (see the bottom illustration at right on the facing page).

4 Once the screen is in position, secure it to the sieve with wire screen staples (F). Use eight staples along each of the ends and then along each of the sides. As you hammer in the staples, keep the screen in position and as taut as possible.

5 When the wire screen is in place, install the four bottom boards. Attach both the shorter bottom boards (C) and the longer bottom boards (D) with three wood screws each. When installing the wood screws along the bottom boards, locate the screw holes so the screws miss the staples and wire screen.

6 Once the bottom boards are fastened, lightly sand the sieve and finish with an exterior stain or paint. If you paint the sieve, be sure to apply an exterior sealer/primer coat first. Once the finish is completely dry, your new Garden Sieve will be ready for service.

The sieve's 30-in. length allows it to be placed across a wheelbarrow or garden cart for easy filling.

Garden Sieve grid pattern

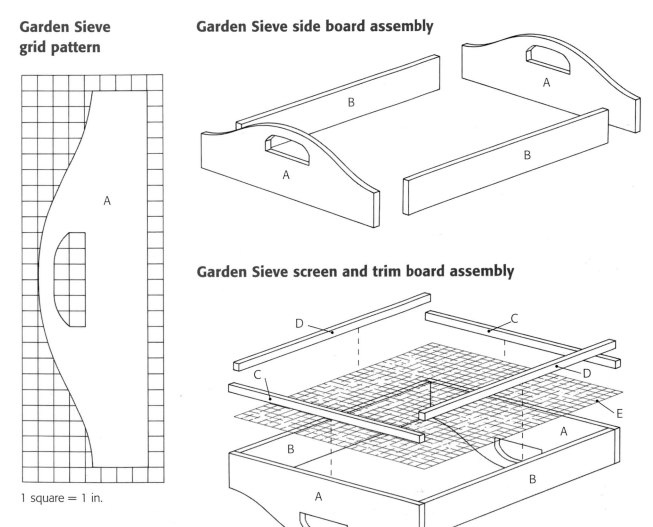

1 square = 1 in.

Garden Sieve side board assembly

Garden Sieve screen and trim board assembly

Vegetables neatly planted in straight rows or geometric patterns make a gar–den look skillfully planned and well organized. Years ago, gardeners achieved precise, crisp lines in their gardens with the help of a line and reel row marker tool. This handy metal device is rarely found in garden stores today, but its design can be easily replicated in wood.

You'll find this tool indispensable at planting time, and its simple design makes it easy to construct. We attached reproduction antique brass hardware to the reel and stake as a finishing touch. To make perfectly straight rows, paths, or planting lines, start by plunging the line stake into the soil. Then reel out the line to your desired length, secure the turnbuckle, and plunge the reel stake into the soil. You're now ready to plant along the line or mark the edges for an impeccably precise path or garden bed.

Creating straight lines for garden beds, paths, and vegetable rows is easily accomplished with this handy Line and Reel Row Marker.

LINE AND REEL ROW MARKER MATERIALS LIST

Key	Qty.	Description	Finished Dimensions	Material
A	1	Reel	3½ in. x 5 in.	Oak
B	1	Reel stake	¾ in. x ¾ in. x 9 in.	Oak
C	1	Line stake	¾ in. x ¾ in. x 14 in.	Oak
D	1	Reel tube	3⁄16 in. (I.D.) x 5 in.	Brass
E	1	Threaded rod	10/32 x 7¼ in.	Brass
F	1	Threaded rod	10/32 x 2¼ in.	Brass
G*	2	Brass drawer pulls	10/32 threading	Brass
H*	1	Turnbuckle	¾ in.	Brass
I	1	Turnbuckle screw	#6 x ¾ in. wood screw	Brass
J	1	Turn knob	¾ in. x ¾ in.	Oak (or similar)
K	1	Turn knob screw	#6 x 1½ in. wood screw	Brass
L	1	String	25 ft.	Nylon

*See project resources on p. 179.

The decorative brass hardware on this project will never rust.

We made our Line and Reel Row Marker out of oak for durability and strength, but you could substitute any clear grade of wood. The style of drawer pull and turn knob can also be easily changed to suit your preference. Find a drawer pull that accepts a 10/32 threaded rod. As the reel turns, this heavier gauge is less likely to bend.

1 Start by cutting out the reel (A) using the grid pattern in the illustration at left on the facing page.

2 Using a 6-in.-long, 7⁄32-in. drill bit, drill a hole through the center of the reel to accept the brass reel tube (see the illustration at right on the facing page).

The Line and Reel Row Marker ensures a straight row and neatly winds in the string when you're finished.

Line and Reel Row Marker grid pattern

A

1 square = ½ in.

Line and Reel Row Marker reel tube assembly

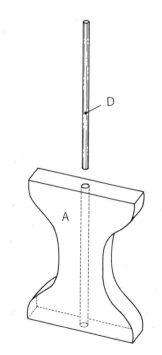

A drill guide will be necessary to ensure that the bit stays centered and straight as you drill (a doweling jig works well). Slip the reel tube (D) into the hole in the reel.

3 Cut out the reel stake (B) and the line stake (C), as shown in the illustrations at right and at left on the facing page. The reel, reel stake, and line stake can all be cut from a standard 2-ft. piece of 1x4 stock. Cut a point at one end of each stake. Round over the opposite end of the line stake with sandpaper as shown, but leave the other end of the reel stake squared off.

4 Use a drill guide and a ⅛-in. drill bit to drill a 2-in.-deep hole in the squared-off or rounded end of each stake as shown.

5 Next, use a ¹⁄₁₆-in. drill bit to make the string (L) tie-off holes in the reel and line stakes (see the illustrations at right and at right on the facing page).

6 Before assembling the pieces, sand and apply an exterior-grade protective finish. We used an oil-based stain on our row marker. Allow the finish to thoroughly dry.

7 Put a few drops of glue in the reel stake hole, then screw one of the drawer pulls (G) onto the threaded rod (E). Insert the other end of the rod through the reel tube and begin to screw the end into the reel stake (see the illustration at left on the facing page). Leave a slight gap between the reel and the drawer pull to allow the reel to spin freely.

8 Screw the other drawer pull onto the shorter threaded rod (F). Put a few drops of glue in the line stake hole, then

screw in the drawer pull until it is snug against the top of the stake (see the illustration below).

9 Next, install the brass turnbuckle (H) and the turn knob (J). The turnbuckle is attached with a small flat-head brass screw (I), while the turn knob is held in place with a longer round-head brass screw (K). Again, leave a slight gap between the head of the screw and the turn knob to allow the knob to rotate freely (see the illustration at right on the facing page).

Line and Reel Row Marker line stake assembly

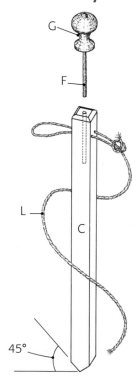

Line and Reel Row Marker
reel stake assembly

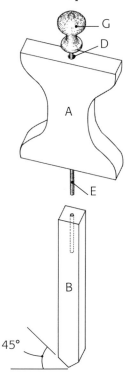

Hardware and string
assembly on reel stake

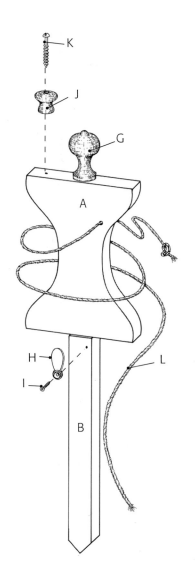

10 Finally, thread one end of the string (L) through the line stake and tie it off as shown in the illustration on the facing page. Thread the other end through the reel and make a knot to prevent it from being pulled back through (see the illustration at right). Wind the string around the reel in a clockwise direction (looking from the top) as shown.

To use the row marker in the garden, first plunge the line stake into the ground at one end of the row. Then move the turnbuckle so it is pointing down and out of the path of the reel. Walk to the other end of your row, letting the string unwind from the reel. When you're ready to mark the other

end, move the turnbuckle to the up position to prevent the reel from turning any further and plunge the reel and stake into the ground. When the row has been planted, move the turnbuckle down and use the turn knob to wind in a counterclockwise direction until the string is wrapped around the reel.

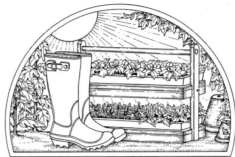

When winter finally yields to spring, gardeners are faced with an escalating number of outdoor chores. To accomplish all of these jobs, gardeners make countless trips back and forth to the garden, tool shed, and cold frame. We designed this Plant Caddy to economize on the number of trips needed to prepare a garden for planting. The Plant Caddy enables you to carry two plant flats in one hand, while leaving the other hand free for large tools such as a rake, hoe, or watering can. With a quick adjustment, the top shelf inverts and becomes a tray for carrying small supplies such as seed packets, pruning shears, twine, or plant tags, while the bottom shelf still has room for a plant flat. Depending on the size of your garden, consider making two Plant Caddies to further reduce the number of trips.

The simple design of the Plant Caddy consists of two trays supported by a handle assembly. All of the wood used

During the busy planting season, this Plant Caddy allows you to carry seeds, seedlings, tools, and supplies to the garden in a single trip.

PLANT CADDY MATERIALS LIST

Key	Qty.	Description	Finished Dimensions	Material
A	2	Handle boards	¾ in. x 2½ in. x 18 in.	Poplar or oak
B	1	Handle dowel	1 in. x 24 in.	Hardwood dowel
C	4	Tray side boards	¾ in. x 1½ in. x 21½ in.	Poplar or oak
D	4	Tray end boards	¾ in. x 1½ in. x 11½ in.	Poplar or oak
E	6	Tray bottom boards	¾ in. x 3½ in. x 23 in.	Poplar or oak
F*	2	Knurled knob bolts	¼-20 x 1 in.	Brass
G	2	Threaded inserst	¼-20	Brass
H	44	Wood screws	#8 x 2 in.	Galvanized
I	6	Wood screws	#7 x 1¼ in.	Galvanized

*See project resources on p. 179.

The top tray quickly inverts to become a second shelf for carrying two plant flats at once.

to make this project is left in standard widths, so a minimal amount of cutting is required. We constructed this project from poplar, but oak would be another good choice.

1 After cutting all of the wood pieces to size, create the two handle boards (A) on a table saw. You can use a dado blade to make the rabbets on each handle board, but we used a standard crosscut blade to slowly "nibble" out the notches. (In other words, we made several narrow cuts with the sawblade instead of a few wide cuts that a dado blade would make.) As shown in the top illustration on the facing page, the two upper notches that accept the removable tray are slightly deeper than the lower notches. This will ensure that the tray can be removed with less binding. It's also a good idea to cut the height of the notch slightly full for the same reason.

2 After notching the two handle boards, drill a 1-in. hole near the top of each board, as shown in the illustration at right. Also cut a ½-in. chamfer, as indicated, to eliminate the sharp corners. With a rubber mallet, tap the length of handle dowel (B) into the two handle boards until the dowel is flush with the two outside surfaces. Once the caddy is complete, you can permanently secure the dowel in place by nailing two small finishing nails through the sides of each handle board into the dowel.

3 After the handle is assembled, make the two trays as shown in the illustration below. Create the frame for each tray by attaching the two tray end boards (D) to the two side boards (C) with two wood screws (H) at each cor-ner. If available, use a miter clamp to keep the frame square. Once the frame is done, attach the three tray bottom boards (E) to one side of the tray frame as shown. Use two wood screws (H) at each end of the middle board and five

Plant Caddy handle assembly

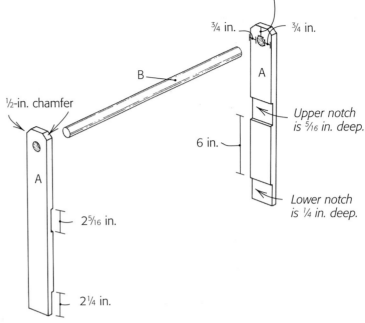

Plant Caddy tray assembly

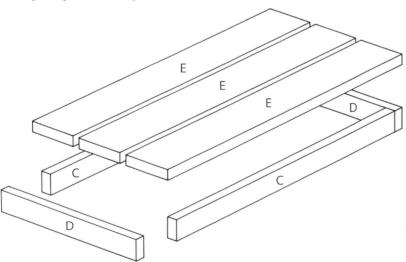

Plant Caddy bottom tray and handle assembly

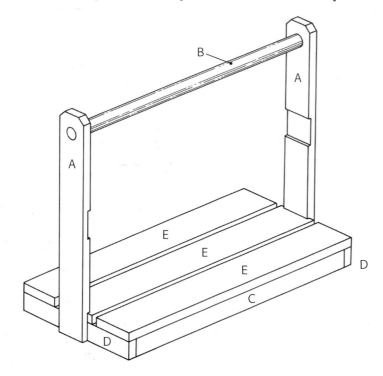

screws on each outside board (one at both ends and three along the out-side edges).

4 Once the two trays are assembled, set one aside to use as the removable top tray. Permanently fix the other tray to the caddy handle boards as shown in the illustration at left. Use three wood screws (I) to attach each end of the handle boards (A) to the bottom tray. Be sure to center the bottom tray and keep the handle boards perpendicular to the tray while installing the wood screws.

5 Locate a midpoint on each end of the top tray where you will install the threaded inserts (G). Measure this mid-point from side to side, as well as from the top edge of the tray end board (D) to the bottom edge of the tray bottom

Inserting the top tray on the Plant Caddy

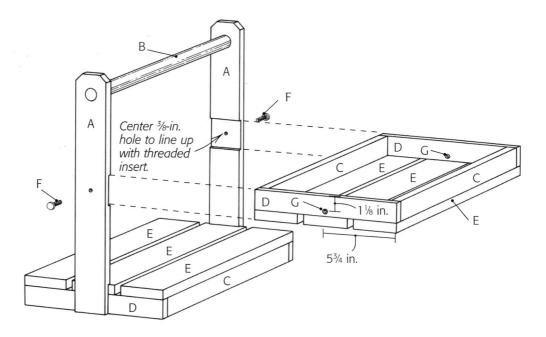

Center ⅜-in. hole to line up with threaded insert.

1⅛ in.

5¾ in.

board (E) (see the bottom illustration on the facing page). Drill the correct size mounting hole in the ends of each tray and use a straight-tipped screwdriver to install the threaded insert (check the specifications for the inserts you purchase to determine the correct size hole to drill).

6 Slide the top tray into the notches cut in the two handle boards. The tray should slide in smoothly. If the fit is too tight, use a rubber mallet to slightly spread the handle boards by tapping them near the handle dowel. If the tray is too loose, tap the handles closer together.

7 With the top tray in place, use a sharp pencil or nail to mark the center point in both handle notches where you will drill a ⅜-in. hole for the two decorative knurled knobs bolts (F). Make the mark through the center of the threaded insert to ensure proper alignment. Remove the top tray and drill both holes.

8 Reinstall the top tray to double-check the hole alignment. The top tray will be held firmly in place once the knurled knobs are inserted through the handle boards and tightened into both ends of the tray (see the bottom illustration on the facing page).

9 Once you are satisfied with the way the top tray slides into place, remove it and apply a finish of your choice. We protected our Plant Caddy with a coat of oil-based stain. Additional coats every two or three years should keep this handy garden accessory in great shape for years to come.

To invert the top tray, simply remove the knurled knob bolt on each end of the Plant Caddy and slide the tray out.

Growing your own annuals and perennials from seed costs a fraction of purchasing the same number of plants from a nursery. If you start more than a flat or two of seedlings every spring, consider making this Flat and Flat Dibble for fast and accurate seed placement.

The Flat Dibble fits standard 11-in. by 22-in. plastic seed trays or the Flat pictured at left. Simply fill your trays with planting medium and press the dibble into the soil, which makes 13 evenly spaced impressions that allow you to accurately sprinkle the seeds along the furrows. As the seedlings grow, air can easily circulate around the evenly spaced sprouts, thereby reducing the risk of damping off. The seedlings are also easier to transplant because their roots are less entwined. Consider making this timesaving tool this winter to produce an abundance of healthy seedlings next spring.

> Speed the process of growing your own seedlings with this handy Flat and Flat Dibble.

FLAT AND FLAT DIBBLE MATERIALS LIST

Key	Qty.	Description	Finished Dimensions	Material
Flat				
A	2	End boards	¾ in. x 2½ in. x 11⅝ in.	Poplar, pine, or oak
B	2	Side boards	¾ in. x 2½ in. x 20½ in.	Poplar, pine, or oak
C	4	Bottom boards	⁵⁄₁₆ in. x 2¾ in. x 22 in.	Poplar, pine, or oak
D	8	Wood screws	#8 x 2 in.	Galvanized
E	18	Wood screws	#7 x 1¼ in.	Galvanized
Flat Dibble				
A	2	End boards	¾ in. x 1½ in. x 11 in.	Poplar, pine, or oak
B	2	Side boards	¾ in. x 1½ in. x 20 in.	Poplar, pine, or oak
C	13	Dibble blades	¼ in. x 2½ in. x 10 in.	Poplar, pine, or oak
D	1	Handle board	¾ in. x 1½ in. x 21½ in.	Poplar, pine, or oak
E	10	Wood screws	#8 x 2 in.	Galvanized

FLAT ASSEMBLY

The Flat and Flat Dibble are constructed from standard–size boards available at most lumberyards or home centers. While we made ours out of poplar, almost any clear wood will work. The Flat is put together much the same as the Plant Caddy trays, however the bottom boards of the Flat are not as thick. To create the ⁵⁄₁₆–in. bottom boards (C), use a table saw to rip standard ¾–in.–thick boards in half (the sawblade cut takes up ⅛ in. of thickness).

1 Start by cutting all of the wood to size. Although thinner than called for, standard ¼–in.–thick boards can be substituted for the ripped bottom boards.

2 Create the frame by attaching the two end boards (A) to the two side boards (B) with two wood screws (D) at each corner (see the illustration on the facing page). If available, use a miter clamp to keep the frame square. Predrill and countersink all screw holes to ensure that the screw heads sit below the surface of the wood.

3 Next, attach the four bottom boards (C) to one side of the tray as shown. Use two wood screws (E) at each end of the two middle boards and five screws on each outside board (one at both ends and three along the outside edges).

4 Sand the Flat smooth and finish with an exterior oil–based stain or wood preservative. Check the label to make sure the finish is nontoxic when cured.

Flat and Flat Dibble flat assembly

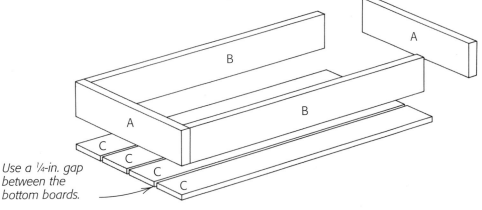

Use a ¼-in. gap between the bottom boards.

FLAT DIBBLE ASSEMBLY

Most lumberyards have a hobby or craft wood section that includes clear grades of oak, poplar, and pine. Unlike standard dimensional lumber, they are often sold in ¼-in., ½-in., and ¾-in. dimensions. The Flat Dibble takes advantage of these thinner sizes to reduce the amount of cutting necessary.

1 After cutting all of the boards to size, make a series of ¼-in.–wide grooves on the inside faces of the side boards (B), as shown in the illustration on p. 164. Clamp the two side boards together (side by side) and run them through the table saw together. By doing so, the grooves on both side boards will line up accurately. Each groove will require two or three passes through the sawblade depending on the thickness (or kerf) of the blade. As you complete each groove, check its width with one of the dibble blades (C). The blade should fit snugly into the groove without forcing. It's a good idea to cut the groove a little too narrow than too wide, as you can't put any material back! If the blade doesn't slide in, trim a bit more until it does.

2 Next, cut the notches in the two end boards (A) that will accept the handle board (D). Make these notches in the same way that you cut the side board grooves. Clamp the two end boards together (side by side) to run them through the saw. It will take several passes through the saw to "nibble" away the ¾-in. notch.

3 To make the bevel on the bottom of the dibble blades, tilt the sawblade to a 45° angle. Adjust the rip fence to make a ⅛-in. bevel cut along one end of the dibble blade. Flip the dibble blade over and cut the opposite bevel. You should end up with a pointed edge along one side of the dibble blade (see the illustration below).

4 Before assembling the dibble blades in the side boards, apply a finish of your choice. Once the frame is assembled, it is difficult to get a brush between the blades.

5 When the finish is dry, assemble the frame. Apply a small amount of waterproof wood glue to the grooves in both

Flat and Flat Dibble dibble assembly

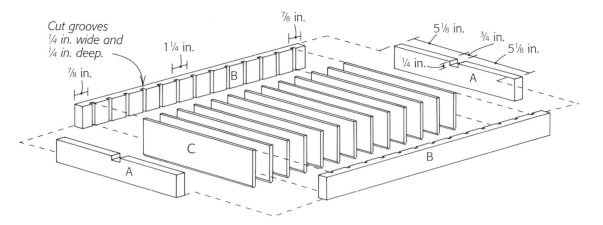

Cut grooves ¼ in. wide and ¼ in. deep.

7⁄8 in.
1¼ in.
7⁄8 in.
5⅛ in.
¾ in.
5⅛ in.
¼ in.

A B C A B

Flat and Flat Dibble handle assembly

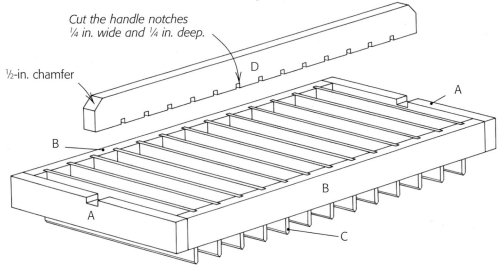

Cut the handle notches
¼ in. wide and ¼ in. deep.

½-in. chamfer

D

A

B

B

A

C

side boards. Fit the dibble blades into the grooves so that the tops of the blades are flush with the tops of the side boards (see the illustration above). Insert each blade into one side board first and then into the other. If necessary, use a rubber mallet to coax the blades into position.

6 Attach the two end boards with two wood screws (E) at each corner. Predrill and countersink all of the screw holes. The wood glue should hold the dibble blades securely in the frame, but if you find one coming loose, secure it with a small brad or escutcheon pin hammered through the side board.

7 To prepare the handle board (D) for installation, set the handle board on the frame and pencil mark the location of all of the dibble blades. Cut out the set of notches in the same way you cut the grooves in the side boards. Also, cut a ½-in. chamfer at both ends of the

handle, as shown in the illustration above. Place the handle on the frame to make sure the dibble blades fit into the handle notches.

8 Before installing the handle board, apply the same finish used on the rest of the Flat Dibble. When dry, install the handle on the frame, carefully working the blades into the handle notches. When the handle is seated properly, secure it with two wood screws from the undersides of the two end boards. Again, predrill and countersink the screw holes.

The Flat and Flat Dibble is now ready to speed the job of seeding a flat by producing a series of straight, crisp furrows. Several flats can be prepared in a fraction of the time it would take without this handy tool.

Enthusiastic gardeners know how quickly a collection of seeds can accumulate. They come from prior seed orders, seed exchanges with friends, and seeds collected from your own garden. This large amount of seed can rapidly overflow even the most generously sized shoebox. The answer is this Seed Saver's Box and uniform seed packets.

This decorative box will neatly organize your collection into three sections. The customized seed packets keep your inventory dated and labeled. In addition, the box will also accommodate most standard seed packet sizes. Perfect for you or as a gift for a gardening friend, the Seed Saver's Box will help make next year's garden planning an enjoyable and organized process.

The Seed Saver's Box uses a locking rabbet joint that is very strong and easy to make on a table-mounted router or table saw. The corners are held together with wood glue and small finishing nails

Keep your collection of seeds dry and well organized in this Seed Saver's Box or consider making one as a gift for a gardening friend.

SEED SAVER'S BOX MATERIALS LIST

Key	Qty.	Description	Finished Dimensions	Material
A	2	Box end boards	¾ in. x 5½ in. x 11½ in.	Oak
B	2	Box side boards	¾ in. x 5½ in. x 15¼ in.	Oak
C	1	Box bottom board	¼ in. x 11 in. x 14¼ in.	Oak-veneered plywood
D	2	Lid end boards	¾ in. x 1½ in. x 11½ in.	Oak
E	2	Lid side boards	¾ in. x 1½ in. x 15¼ in.	Oak
F	1	Lid glass	¹⁄₁₆ in. x 10⅞ in. x 14⅛ in.	Window glass
G	2	Lid trim molding	⅜ in. x ¾ in. x 12 in.	Oak (half-round or equivalent)
H	2	Lid trim molding	⅜ in. x ¾ in. x 15¼ in.	Oak (half-round or equivalent)
I	2	Box dividers	¼ in. x 5¼ in. x 10½ in.	Poplar
J	2	Box dividers	¼ in. x 5¼ in. x 13¾ in.	Poplar
K	2	Box dividers	¼ in. x 5¼ in. x 10¼ in.	Poplar
L	16	Finishing nails	4d (1½ in.)	Galvanized
M	12	Escutcheon pins	18 x ¾ in.	Brass
N*	2	Hinges	1⁵⁄₁₆ in. x 2¼ in.	Brass (with screws)
O*	1	Lid knob	¼ in. x ¾ in.	Brass
P	2	Lid chain	³⁄₁₆ in. x 12 in.	Brass
Q	4	Lid chain screws	#4 x ⅝ in.	Brass

*See project resources on p. 179.

Made from oak and appointed with brass hardware and an etched glass top, this seed box is attractive enough to display.

Seed Saver's Box side board assembly

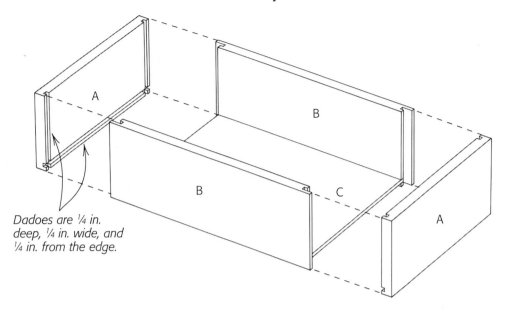

Dadoes are ¼ in. deep, ¼ in. wide, and ¼ in. from the edge.

A

B

B

C

A

to ensure that the seams will never loosen. We also included a glass top with a decorative etched pattern. For protection against moisture, add a few packets of silica desiccant to keep your seeds dry and ready for the next planting season.

1 Cut all of the box and lid boards to size, except for the lid trim molding and box dividers.

2 Using a table–mounted router with a ¼-in. straight bit, cut the joint profiles shown in the illustration above. (You can also use a table saw by making two or three passes for each dado.) Start with the two box end boards (A) and make a dado on each end of the boards ¼ in. deep and ¼ in. wide.

3 With the same fence setting, also make a lengthwise dado on the end boards (A) and side boards (B). This dado will accept the bottom board (C) when you assemble the four sides of the box.

4 Next, cut the end profile of side boards (B). Position each side board vertically against the fence and pass it through the router with the bit set to a

Seed Saver's Box cutting profile for side board (B)

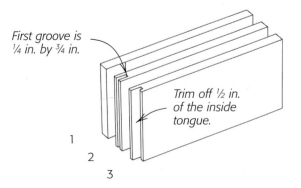

First groove is ¼ in. by ¾ in.

Trim off ½ in. of the inside tongue.

1

2

3

Seed Saver's Box joint assembly

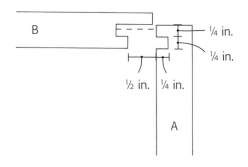

height of ¾ in. This creates two equal-length tongues on the end of the board. Repeat this step for all four ends of the side boards. Complete this profile by lowering the bit to a height of ¼ in. and trimming ½ in. of the tongue that will be on the inside of the box (see the bottom illustration on p. 169). The four sides of the box should look as shown in the illustration above.

5 Repeat steps 2 through 4 for the lid end boards (D) and side boards (E) (see the illustration below). Instead of mak-

ing a dado for the bottom board, cut a rabbet along the top inside edge of the lid boards to accept the sheet of lid glass (F). The rabbet should be ¹⁄₁₆ in. deep (or the same thickness as the glass you use) and ¼ in. wide.

6 After checking the assembly of the box with a trial fit, put a bead of wood glue along the lower dado of the box side boards (B). Insert the bottom board (C) into the two dadoes on the side boards, as shown in the top illustration on p. 169. Next, put a bead of glue along the lower dado of the box end boards (A) as well as on the inner surfaces of the corner rabbet joints. Install the box end boards as shown. Wipe off any excess glue and hold the pieces in place with bar clamps. Let the box assembly sit overnight so the glue can completely dry.

7 Glue and clamp the four lid boards (D, E) and set aside to dry overnight.

8 To ensure that the corners of the box and lid stay tight, nail three 4d finishing nails (L) at each corner of the box

Seed Saver's Box lid assembly

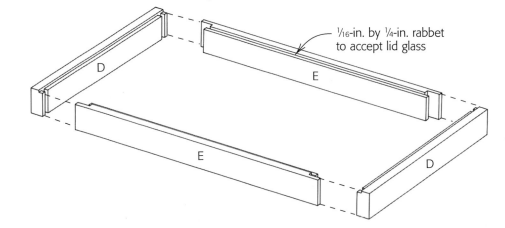

¹⁄₁₆-in. by ¼-in. rabbet to accept lid glass

and one at each corner of the lid, nailing them through the side boards and into the end boards. Countersink the nail heads (see the photo on p. 168).

9 Once the box and lid are complete, cut to size the six box dividers (I, J, K). We recommend cutting the length of each divider about 1 in. longer than needed, then pencil marking the exact length while holding it in position.

10 With the dividers cut roughly to length, cut the double chamfer along the top edge of each board to create a pointed ridge (see the illustration at right).

11 Next, cut a 45° bevel on each end of the four outside divider boards (I, J). While you're cutting the corner bevels, you will also be cutting these boards to their exact lengths in order to fit snugly inside the box.

12 Test the fit of the outside divider boards inside the box. Remove the two dividers (J) and cut two dadoes on each board, as shown in the illustration at right. These dadoes accept the middle divider boards (K). Cut the middle dividers to their final length and slide them into place.

13 Apply a protective finish to the box, lid, and divider boards, then set it aside to dry. We applied an oil-based stain to our seed box.

14 Once the finish is dry, set the lid on the box. Before installing the lid glass (F), we decided to add a decorative touch by etching a pattern on the surface.

Seed Saver's Box insert assembly

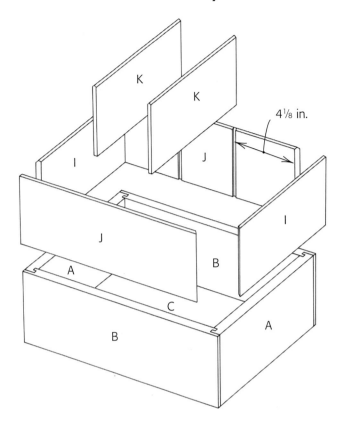

4⅛ in.

Etching cream is easy to use and can be found at most craft stores. You can apply contact paper to the glass as we did, or purchase one of the many precut stencils that are available. If you decide to use etching cream, carefully follow all directions.

15 Set the lid glass into position, as shown in the top illustration on p. 172. The glass is held in place by the lid molding pieces (G, H). Using a miter box, cut the four lid trim molding pieces to size. Check the length of each piece against the top edge of the box before cutting. Once you are satisfied that all

Seed Saver's Box lid glass and trim molding assembly

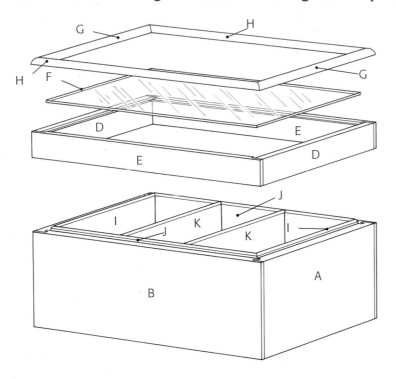

Seed Saver's Box hinge, chain, and knob assembly

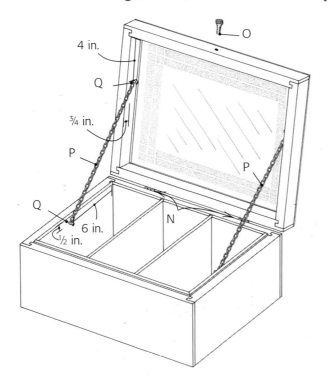

four pieces properly fit on top of the lid, nail them in place with brass escutcheon pins (M). Predrill to prevent the wood from splitting.

16 When the lid is completed, add the decorative brass hinges (N). Check the motion of the lid as it opens and closes–it should move smoothly and seat squarely on the top of the box.

17 Next, add the brass lid knob (O) to the front of the lid (see the bottom illustration at left). We simply pushed the knob into a ¼-in. hole coated with wood glue.

18 To install the lid chains (P), drill two pilot holes for the brass screws (Q) that anchor the chain to the lid (see the bottom illustration at left). Attach the other ends of the chains to the box dividers (I) using the remaining two brass screws (you may need to temporarily remove the two inside divider boards to install these screws).

Once you have finished, fill your Seed Saver's Box with all those seed packets left over from past gardens. Better yet, make your own seed packets (see the sidebar on the facing page) and face the next growing season completely organized.

If you collect seeds from your garden, these customized seed packets will keep your collection organized and ready for next year's planting. Each packet has designated lines for labeling the plant name, the date the seed was collected, and its origin, whether it's your backyard, a friend's garden, or perhaps the name of a catalog if you have seeds left over from a previous year's order.

To create the seed packets, start by making photocopies of the illustration on p. 174. If you plan to collect a wide variety of seeds, consider using several paper colors to organize your inventory. For example, choose one color for packets containing annual flowers, another color for perennial flowers, and a third for vegetables. Next, carefully cut out the pattern just inside the line so that no black ink remains around the perimeter. Then along the lines provided, fold over the back of the seed packet, followed by the side and bottom flaps. Use rubber cement to glue the bottom and side flap to the back of the seed packet. Once you've filled the packet with seeds, fold over the rounded top flap and secure it with rubber cement.

These seed packets not only keep your seeds organized but also make wonderful homemade gifts for gardening friends. In early autumn, fill five or six packets with seeds from your favorite flowers and vegetables and fill out the front labels. Stack the packets on top of each other and tie the bundle with ribbon or raffia. It's a gift a gardener will appreciate and remember with each new growing season.

Keep your seeds labeled and organized in these customized seed packets.

Use the seed packets to create special homemade gifts for your gardening friends.

Seed packet pattern

GARDEN
SEEDS

PLANT NAME

ORIGIN

DATE

GLOSSARY

Bevel Any angle cut other than 90°. A bevel may be cut with a table saw, radial arm saw, circular saw, router, or planer.

Chamfer An angle cut made along the edge of a board. A chamfer is usually cut at a 45° angle using a table saw, circular saw, radial arm saw, router, or planer.

Clear Wood A grade of lumber containing very few, if any, knots.

Countersink To use a countersink drill bit to enlarge the upper part of a drill hole to accept the head of a screw so it's flush with or below the wood surface.

Cove Molding A type of molding with a concave face often used to trim the junction between a wall and a ceiling.

Crosscut To cut across the grain of a board.

Cupping The curving of a piece of lumber across its width creating a cup-shape or concave end profile.

Dado A rectangular or square cut across the face of a board to create a groove of any width. To make this cut, use a straight router bit, a radial arm saw, or a table saw fitted with a dado blade.

Doweling Jig A jig used to accurately drill opposing holes in two pieces of wood to accept dowel pins. (See Dowel Joints on p. 63.)

Drill Guide A tool used to accurately guide a drill bit into a board at a 90° angle.

Escutcheon Pins Small brass nails with rounded heads.

Featherboard A safety accessory used on table saws or table-mounted routers. It firmly holds a piece of wood against the guide or rip fence. (See Push Stick and Featherboard on p. 15.)

Finial A decorative ornament at the apex of a structure.

Footprint The area of a structure's base.

Hardwoods Wood coming from broad-leafed trees such as oak or maple. (See Woods on pp. 16–17.)

Kerf The width of a cut made by a sawblade.

Miter An angle cut across a piece of wood. (See Cutting Molding on pp. 30–31.)

Miter Box A plastic or wooden U-shaped box with precut slots on both sides to accurately guide a backsaw in cutting a miter.

Mortise A hollowed-out space in a board, shaped to accept a tenon. (See Mortise and Tenon Joints on p. 77.)

Push Stick A safety accessory used to push wood stock through high-speed sawblades. (See Push Stick and Featherboard on p. 15.)

Rabbet A groove or channel cut along the edge of a board.

Ripping Reducing a board's dimension by cutting or "ripping" it along its grain.

Softwoods Wood coming from coniferous trees such as cedar, redwood, fir, and spruce. (See Woods on pp. 16–17.)

Square When two boards or objects are at right angles to one another. The term can also refer to an L-shaped tool used to check 90° angles (carpenter's square or framer's square).

Taper To gradually decrease in size toward one end, such as with a spire or pyramid.

Tapering Jig A tool used to make uniform tapered cuts. (See instructions on finial construction on pp. 40–42.)

Tenon A projection or tongue cut on one end of a board to fit a matching mortise. (See Mortise-and-Tenon Joints on p. 77.)

Tongue-and-Groove Siding Siding boards that have a groove cut along one edge and a tongue or tenon cut on the other. When placed side by side, the tongue slides into the corresponding groove for an interlocking joint.

RESOURCES

1. The Antique Hardware Store
19 Buckingham Plantation Dr.
Bluffton, SC 29910-6504
1-800-422-9982
http://www.antiquehardware.com

2. Cascade Greenhouse Supply
2626 15th Avenue W.
Seattle, WA 98119
1-800-353-0264

3. Charley's Greenhouse Supply
1599 Memorial Hwy.
Mount Vernon, WA 98273
1-800-322-4707

4. Crown City Hardware Co.
1047 N. Allen Ave.
Pasadena, CA 91104-3298
1-800-816-8492

5. Eagle America
P.O. Box 1099
Chardon, OH 44024
1-800-950-1047

6. Harbor Freight Tools
3491 Mission Oaks Blvd.
Camarillo, CA 93011-6010
1-800-423-2567
http://www.harborfreight.com

7. International Tool Corporation
2590 Davie Rd.
Davie, FL 33317
1-800-338-3384
http://www.internationaltool.com

8. Leichtung Workshops
1108 N. Glenn Rd.
Casper, WY 82601
1-800-321-6840

9. McFeely's Square Drive Screws
P.O. Box 11169
Lynchburg, VA 24506-9963
1-800-443-7937
http://www.mcfeeleys.com

10. NH Northern Lawn & Garden Supply Catalog
P.O. Box 1499
Burnsville, MN 55337-0499
1-800-533-5545
http://www.northern-online.com

11. Tool Crib of the North
P.O. Box 14040
Grand Forks, ND 58208-4040
1-800-358-3096
http://www.toolcribofthenorth.com

12. Trend-Lines
135 American Legion Hwy.
Revere, MA 02151
1-800-767-9999

13. Woodcraft
210 Wood Country Industrial Park
P.O. Box 1686
Parkersburg, WV 26102-1686

14. The Wookworkers' Store
4365 Willow Dr.
Medina, MN 55340
1-800-279-4441

15. Woodworker's Supply
1108 N. Glenn Rd.
Casper, WY 82601
1-800-645-9292

PROJECT RESOURCES

The resources on the facing page carry a variety of tools and supplies. Since it will be helpful for you to know the resources we used for the individual projects, the number following each item corresponds to the number next to each supplier's name. Unless otherwise mentioned, all other project materials can be found at local home centers or lumberyards.

Greenhouse Table (p. 56)
Dowel pins: 14
Iron brackets: 1
Wood plugs: 14
Wood screws: 9

Potting Bench (p. 64)
Hooks: 4
Wood screws: 9

Rolling Bench (p. 70)
Dowel pins: 14
Garden cart wheels: 10
Wood screws: 9

Vegetable Washstand (p. 84)
Cupboard door hardware: 4
Wood screws: 9

Cold Frame (p. 102)
Dowel pins: 14
Glazing tape: 3
Hinges: 14
Wood screws: 9
Vent openers: 2, 3

Strawberry Tower (p. 112)
Dowel pins: 14
Wood screws: 9

Greenhouse (p. 118)
Cement screws: 9
Dowel pins: 14
Glazing tape: 3
Hinges: 14
Lap clips: 3
Vent openers: 2, 3
Wood plugs: 14
Wood screws: 9

Line and Reel Row Marker (p. 148)
Brass drawer pulls: 4
Brass turnbuckle: 14

Plant Caddy (p. 154)
Knurled knob bolt: 14

Seed Saver's Box (p. 166)
Knob: 14
Hinges: 14

BIBLIOGRAPHY

Abram, Norm. *Measure Twice, Cut Once.* New York: Little, Brown and Company, 1996.

Brickell, Christopher, and David Joyce. *The American Horticultural Society Pruning and Training.* New York: Dorling Kindersley, 1996.

Burch, Monte. *How to Build Small Barns & Outbuildings.* Pownal, Vt.: Garden Way Publishing, 1992.

Day, David, Simon Jennings, and Albert Jackson. *The Complete Manual of Woodworking.* New York: Alfred A. Knopf, 1989.

DeCristoforo, R. J. *Woodworking Techniques: Joints and Their Applications.* Reston, Va.: Reston Publishing Company (A Prentice–Hall Co.), 1978.

Duginske, Mark. *Mastering Woodworking Machines.* Newtown, Conn.: The Taunton Press, 1992.

Feirer, John L., and Gilbert R. Hutchings. *Carpentry & Building Construction.* New York: Macmillan Publishing, 1986.

Fine Woodworking on Woodworking Machines. Newtown, Conn.: The Taunton Press, 1985.

Engler, Nick. *Outdoor Furniture.* Emmaus, Pa.: Rodale Press, 1988.

Geary, Don. *Woodworking Projects for the Great Outdoors.* Pownal, Vt.: Garden Way Publishing, 1990.

Huff, Darrell. *How to Work with Concrete and Masonry.* New York: Harper & Row (Popular Science Books), 1968.

Oughton, Frederick. *The Complete Manual of Wood Finishing.* New York: Stein and Day, 1983.

METRIC EQUIVALENCE CHART

Inches	Centimeters	Millimeters	Inches	Centimeters	Millimeters
⅛	0.3	3	13	33.0	330
¼	0.6	6	14	35.6	356
⅜	1.0	10	15	38.1	381
½	1.3	13	16	40.6	406
⅝	1.6	16	17	43.2	432
¾	1.9	19	18	45.7	457
⅞	2.2	22	19	48.3	483
1	2.5	25	20	50.8	508
1¼	3.2	32	21	53.3	533
1½	3.8	38	22	55.9	559
1¾	4.4	44	23	58.4	584
2	5.1	51	24	61.0	610
2½	6.4	64	25	63.5	635
3	7.6	76	26	66.0	660
3½	8.9	89	27	68.6	686
4	10.2	102	28	71.1	711
4½	11.4	114	29	73.7	737
5	12.7	127	30	76.2	762
6	15.2	152	31	78.7	787
7	17.8	178	32	81.3	813
8	20.3	203	33	83.8	838
9	22.9	229	34	86.4	864
10	25.4	254	35	88.9	889
11	27.9	279	36	91.4	914
12	30.5	305			

Publisher: JIM CHILDS

Associate publisher: HELEN ALBERT

Editorial assistant: CHERILYN DeVRIES

Editor: DIANE SINITSKY

Designer/layout artist: LYNNE PHILLIPS

Photographer: MICHAEL GERTLEY

Illustrator: JAN GERTLEY

Typeface: NOFRET, FORMATA

Paper: 80-LB. UTOPIA TWO GLOSS

Printer: R. R. DONNELLEY, WILLARD, OHIO